P.C. Balkrishna

FIGURE DRAWING
for graphics designers

PUSTAK MAHAL®

Publishers
Pustak Mahal®

J-3/16 , Daryaganj, New Delhi-110002
☎ 23276539, 23272783, 23272784
Fax: 011-23260518
E-mail: info@pustakmahal.com
Website: www.pustakmahal.com

Sales Centre
• 10-B, Netaji Subhash Marg, Daryaganj
New Delhi-110002,
☎ 23268292, 23268293, 23279900
Fax: 011-23280567
E-mail: rapidexdelhi@indiatimes.com

• 6686, Khari Baoli, Delhi-110006
☎ 23944314, 23911979

Branches
Bengaluru: ☎ 080-22234025 • *Telefax:* 080-22240209
E-mail: pustak@airtelmail.in
pustak@sancharnet.in
Mumbai: ☎ 022-22010941, 022-22053387
E-mail: rapidex@bom5.vsnl.net.in
Patna: ☎ 0612-3294193 • *Telefax:* 0612-2302719
E-mail: rapidexptn@rediffmail.com
Hyderabad: *Telefax:* 040-24737290
E-mail: pustakmahalhyd@yahoo.co.in

ISBN 978-81-223-1254-6
Edition: 2011

Printed at : Param Offsetters, Okhla, New Delhi-110020

Foreword

Any presentation calls for new ideas and skill in their preparation. Computer Graphics software help a great deal in these projects to convey the message effectively. Animation enhances the impact.

Drawing is a basic instinct. Children begin to draw even before they can write the alphabets. Hence each individual has some skill in drawing.

Many young people, though well-versed in the use of computer software, fall short of the mark due to their drawing ability. There is no need to undergo elaborate training in art.

This book is meant to assist them to make effective sketches which can be incorporated in their presentations.

Basic ideas of animation are also included in this book. Though tweening has become mechanical, physically drawing them is needed when depicting certain movements.

Copy the figures given in this book several times in a sketch-book and try to create your own characters.

Wish you all great success in your designing career.

P.C.Balkrishna

Animation

Let us learn the method and techniques of animation and design our own character for animated cartoon pictures. Let that free hand on paper show its magic on your computer screen to create interesting concepts and plots.

I have found **Macromedia Flash MX** very convenient and easy, both for designing and animation. Though newer versions of Flash have been introduced, Flash MX is simple to use.

Instal Flash in your PC. The screen resolution may be set according to the requirement. If the animation is for TV or cinema higher resolution is needed.

The Flash screen contains:

Menu Bar, Tool Box, Timeline, Stage (a white rectangle), Scene No. Bar.

The picture on the following page will be self explanatory.

For designing characters circles have been used in this book. To get a perfect circle > press down 'Shift' > click and drag.

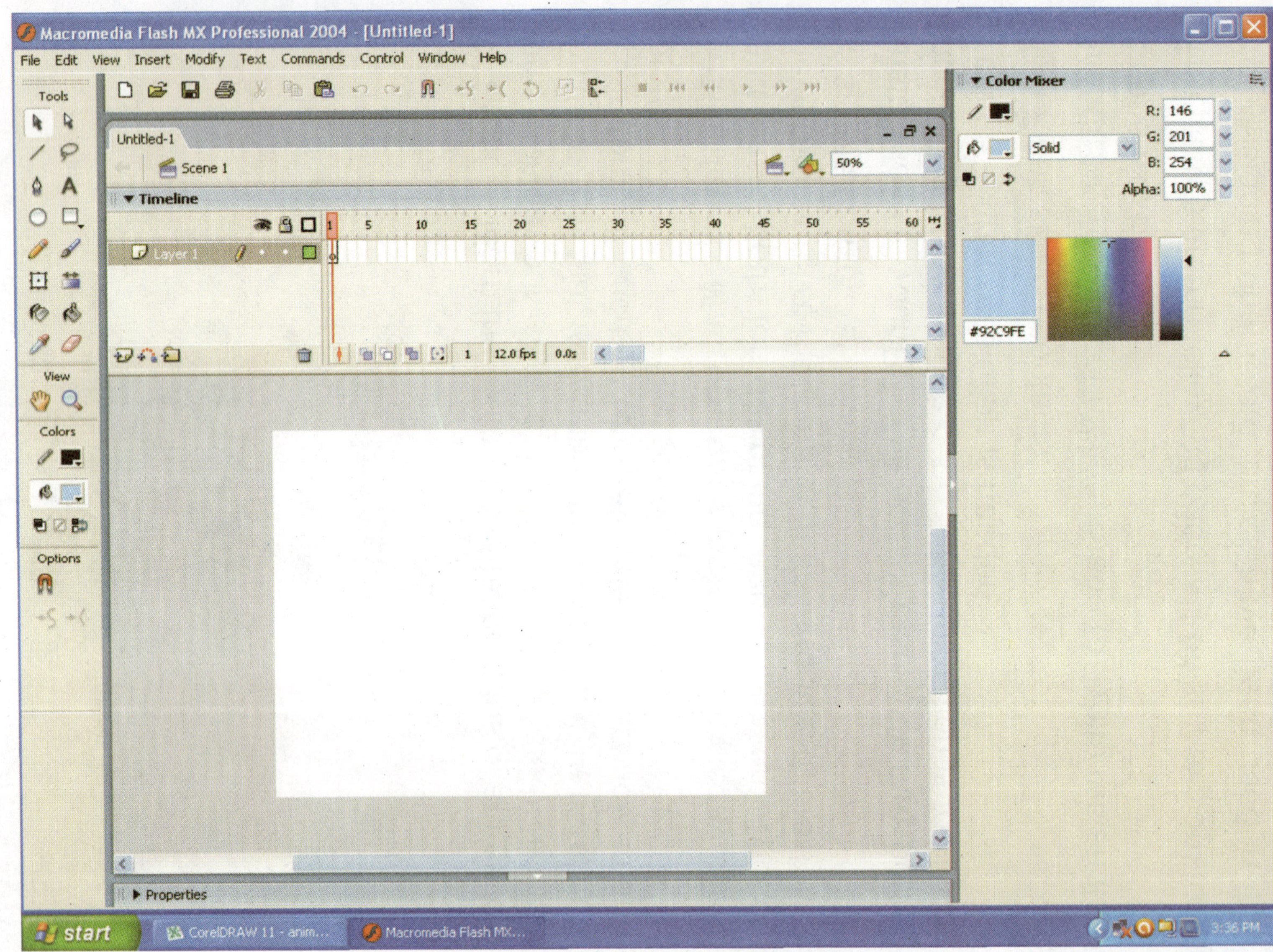
Macromedia Flash MX Professional 2004 - [Untitled-1]
File Edit View Insert Modify Text Commands Control Window Help
Tools
View
Colors
Options
Untitled-1
Scene 1
50%
Timeline
Layer 1
12.0 fps
0.0s
Color Mixer
Solid
R: 146
G: 201
B: 254
Alpha: 100%
#92C9FE
Properties
start
CorelDRAW 11 - anim...
Macromedia Flash MX...
3:36 PM

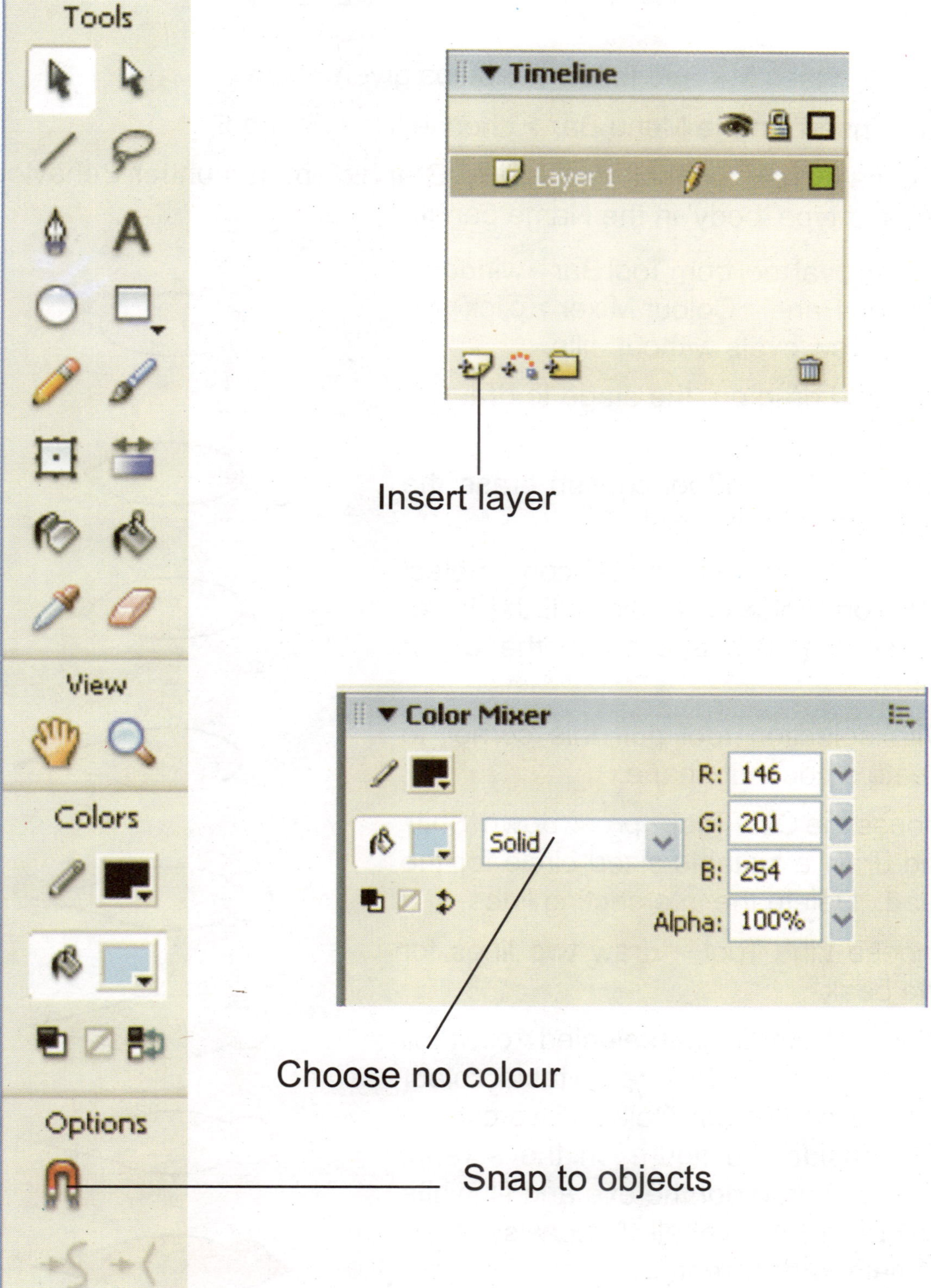
Tools
View
Colors
Options
Timeline
Layer 1
Insert layer
Color Mixer
Solid
R: 146
G: 201
B: 254
Alpha: 100%
Choose no colour
Snap to objects

Draw a bird and make it fly

Open your Flash MX and follow the steps given below:

1. Click 'Insert' on the Menu Bar > choose 'New Symbol'.
2. In 'Create New Symbol' panel click 'Graphic' button under Behaviour List and type 'body' in the Name panel.
3. Choose oval tool from Tool Bar > windows >Design Panel >Colour Mixer > click 'No Fill' to draw ovals without fills.
4. Click and drag on the stage to draw an oval.
5. With the Eraser Tool chosen erase the end portion of the oval.
6. Activate 'Snap to Objects' icon. Select Selection tool > click and pull the lower end so that it snaps on to the upper end.
7. With selection tool pull this corner to create a coconut shape.
8. Choose the Oval Tool > press down 'Shift' and draw a suitable sized circle for the head. Delete the intersecting lines.
9. Choose Line Tool > draw two lines for the beak.
10. With the Paint Bucket selected > click 'Fill Colour' icon > Choose suitable colour for the body from Colour Swatches > click inside the figure on the screen. Remember to dot the eye and fill white colour in the eyeball. Otherwise it will remain transparent.

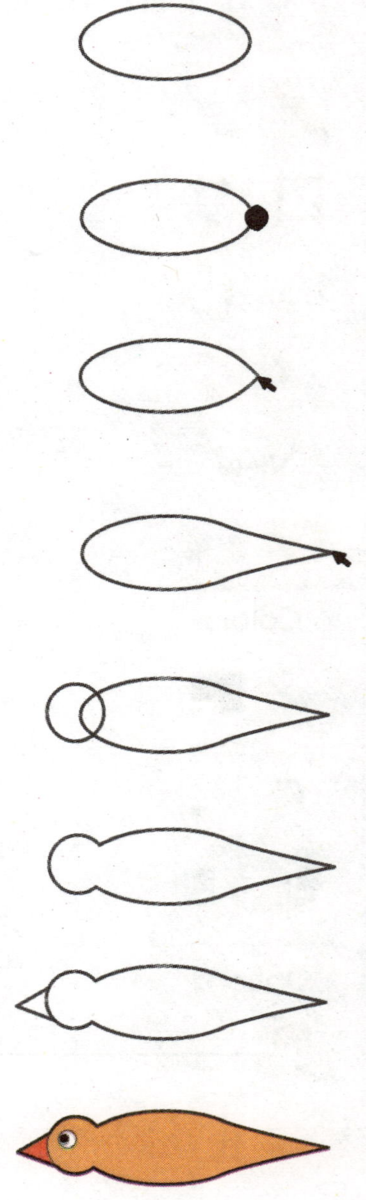

To draw the wings, follow the steps given below:

1. Click 'Insert' on the Menu Bar > New Symbol. For Behaviour, click 'Graphic' as you did for the body. > Type 'wing' in the Name window.

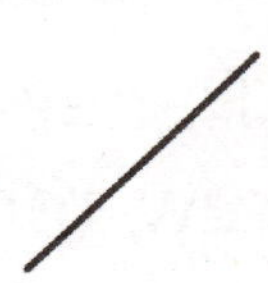

2. Draw an oblique line with the Line tool > nudge it with the Selection Tool as shown.

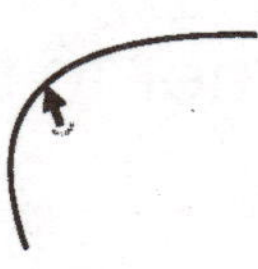

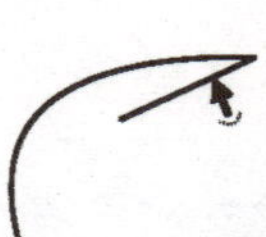

3. Draw a line from the top end of the curve > Shape it with the Selection Tool.

4. Select this line > Press down ctrl+D to get a duplicate > select it and align as shown. Repeat this process to draw all the feathers. Or select the line > press down Alt+D and place the feathers one by one.

5. Close the gap and fill colour and remove the closing line. Both the drawings (symbols) are automatically stored in the library. To get them onto the stage > windows > library >click and drag the picture on to the stage.

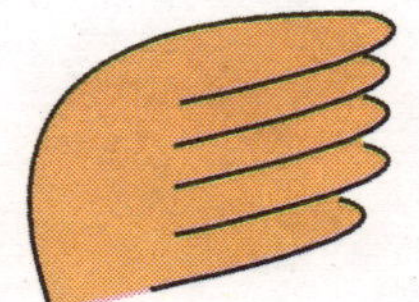

To start the animation click ‘Scene 1’ above the Timeline.

1. Click the first frame on the Timeline to activate it.
2. Choose Rectangle tool from the Tool Box > click ‘Fill Colour’ icon > Choose light blue colour from the swatches.
3. Click 'Windows’ on the Menu Bar > Design Panels > click ‘Colour Mixer’ > click ‘No Colour’ Icon to draw rectangles without borders.
4. On the stage click and drag from the top left corner to the right bottom corner to draw a rectangle.
5. Right click frame 48 on the Timeline > click ‘Insert Frames’. The background for the action is ready.
6. Double click the layer name (layer 1) > type ‘background’ and lock the layer.

7. Add a layer by clicking the ‘Insert Layer’ icon found below the layer name list. Click the first frame of this layer to activate it.
8. Click and drag the instance of the ‘body’ symbol on to the stage and place it in the centre of the stage. Then right click frame 48 on the Timeline > choose ‘Insert Frames’.

9. Double click ‘layer 2’ name > type ‘body’ and lock the layer.

10. Add another layer > name it 'wing' > click first frame of this layer to activate it. From the library click and drag the instance of the wing on to the stage and align it in relation to the body.

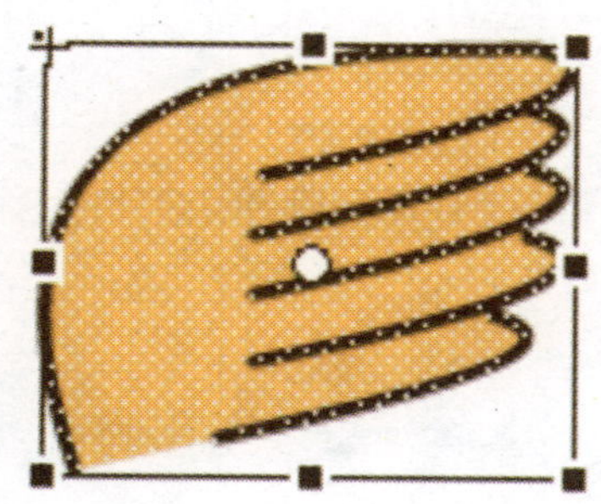

11. Click the 'Free Transform' tool > click the wing on the stage > move the centre of the rectangle to the bottom line.

12. Right click frame 12 of the wing Timeline > click 'insert key frame'. Make sure that the centre point you moved is on the lower side of the rectangle.

13. With the help of the Free Transform tool handle collapse the wing as shown.

14. Right click anywhere between frames 1 and 12 on the 'wing' Timeline > choose 'Insert Motion Tween'.

15. Right click frame 13 on this Timeline > click 'Insert Key Frame' > delete figure on the stage.

16. Click and drag the instance of the 'wing' symbol from the library on to the stage > place it is the precise position. Click

'Modity' on the Menu Bar > Transform > click 'Flip vertical'. Click 'Free Transform' icon on the Tool Box > move the centre of the modifier rectangle to the upper side.

17. Right click frame 24 > click 'Insert Key Frame'.
18. Click frame 13 > collapse the wing upward by moving the modifier handle upward.
19. Right click anywhere between frame 13 and 24 > choose >'insert motion tween'. Then test animation by pressing 'Enter'.

The above 19 steps create the animation to move the wing from the top position to the bottom position. To complete the cycle of flapping of the wing create key frames and tweens to take it from the bottom position to the top position. Test the movie by pressing 'enter'.

1. Create symbols for clouds by using the 'Oval' tool without borders.

2. Keep the colour of the clouds white or off-white.

3. On a separate layer named 'clouds' place the instance of the clouds on the left, outside the stage on frame 1. Right click frame 48 > move the cloud instance to the right out of

the stage > right click any frame between frames 1 and 48 > choose 'Insert Motion Tween'.

4. Click 'Control' on the Menu Bar > choose 'Loop Playback'. Test movie as usual and observe the bird fly on and on and on.

Here are frames from a complete movie

Exhausted and panting Pussy Doctor achieved by using Free Transform tool to distort the chest.

All body parts, stetho, tie, specs, eyes, mouth, coat and sleeves were put on different layers. Shape tweeing was used for mouth and eyes.

The characters designed in this book have been used in the scenes shown here.

If the positions of the duckling and the fish are put on separate frames and Tweens supplied between them, an exciting action will result. Try it.

How to Hold the Pencil

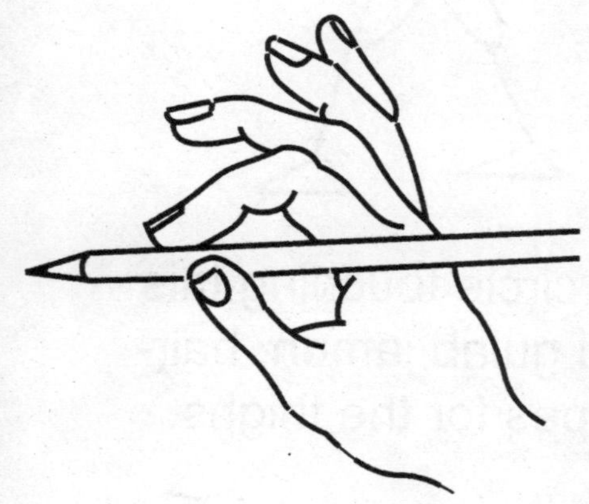

Hold the pencil lightly between the thumb and index finger

and support it with the middle finger.

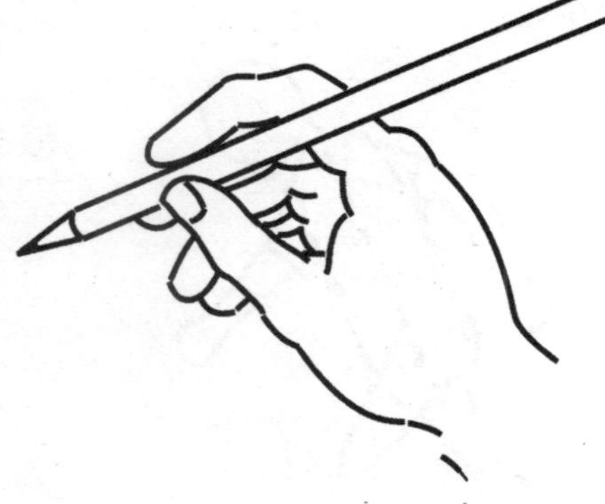

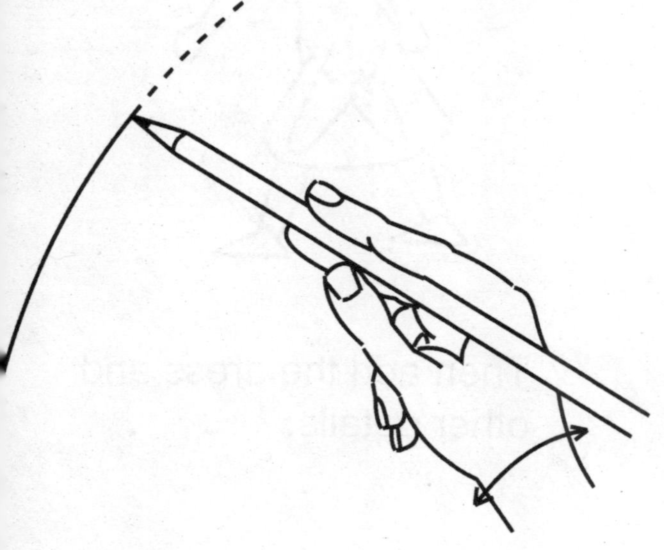

For drawing smooth curves, hold the pencil lightly between the thumb, the index and middle fingers, keeping them straight. Use the movement of the wrist to draw the curves.

Draw an oval in the shape of a gulab jamun and divide it lengthwise by a line.

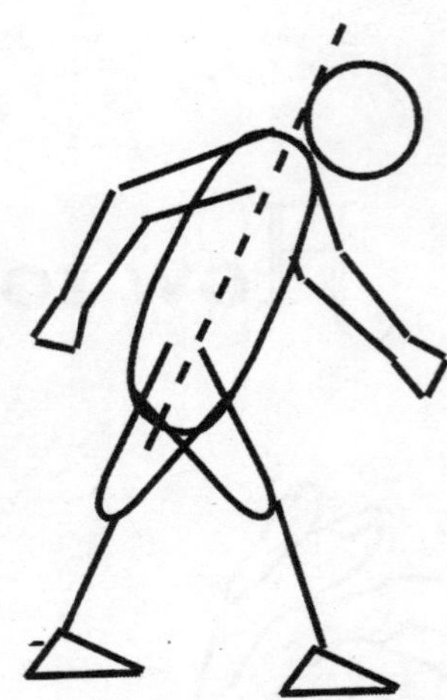

Draw a circle touching this line and gulab jamun, hair-pin shapes for the thighs.

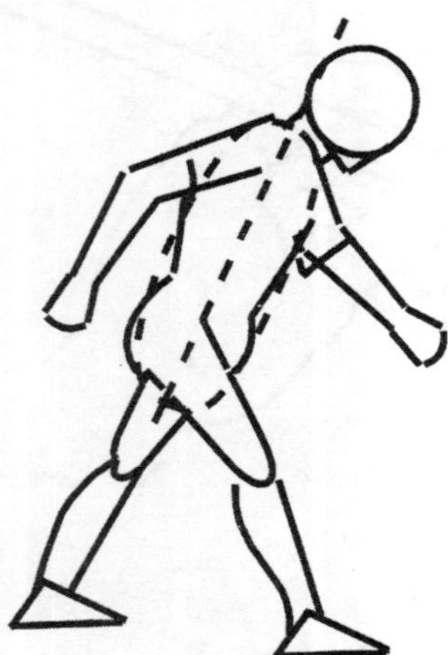

Lines for legs and triangles for feet. Draw lines for arms as shown. Complete the shape first.

Then add the dress and other details.

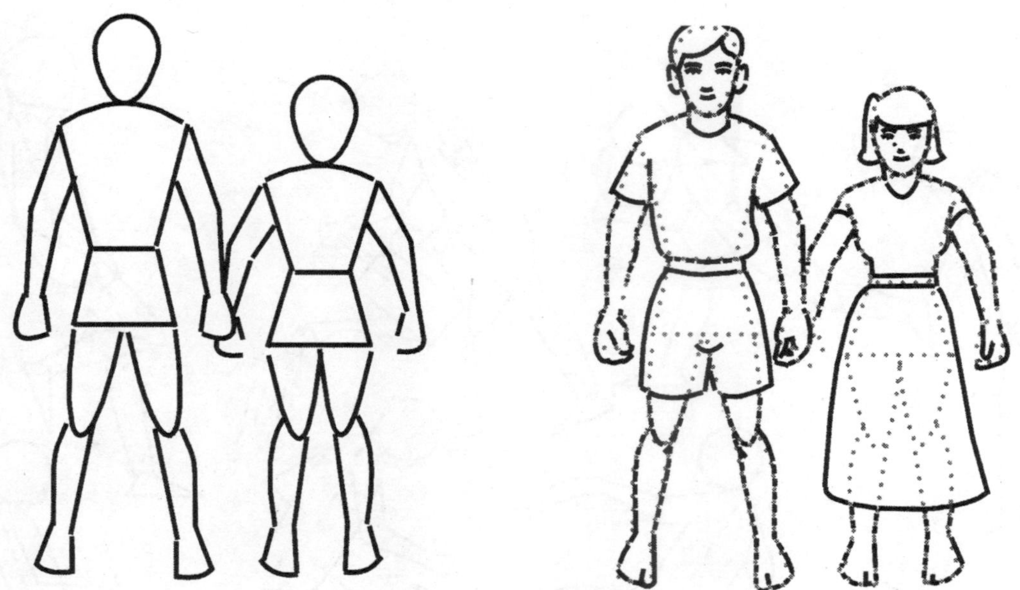

Front view

Draw a bucket shape above an inverted garden pot. Make two hair-pin shapes for the thighs. Draw all the guide lines first, then an oval for the head.
In female figures the bucket is shorter and the garden pot taller.

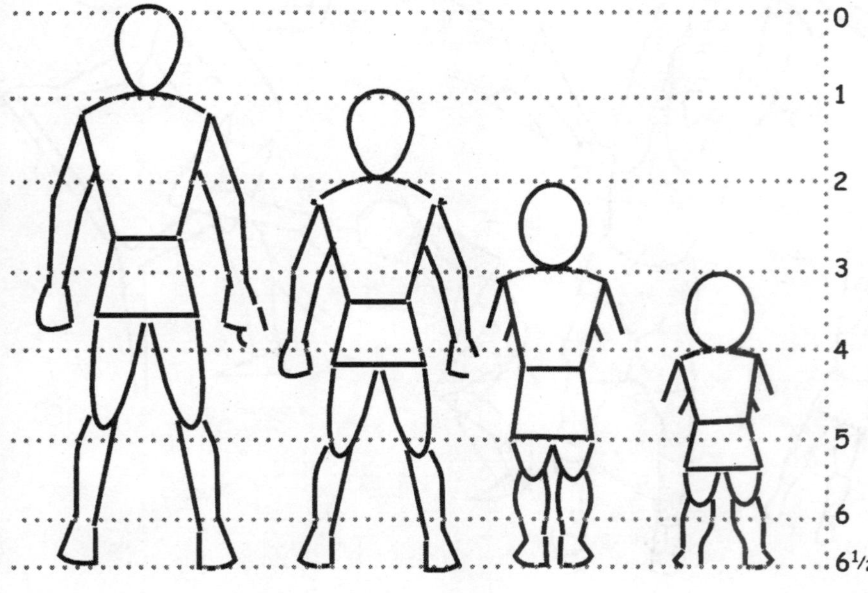

Make use of the size of the head to draw human figures.

An adult is 6½ heads tall, a 10-yr-old is 5 heads tall and 2-yr-old is 3 to 3 ½ heads tall.

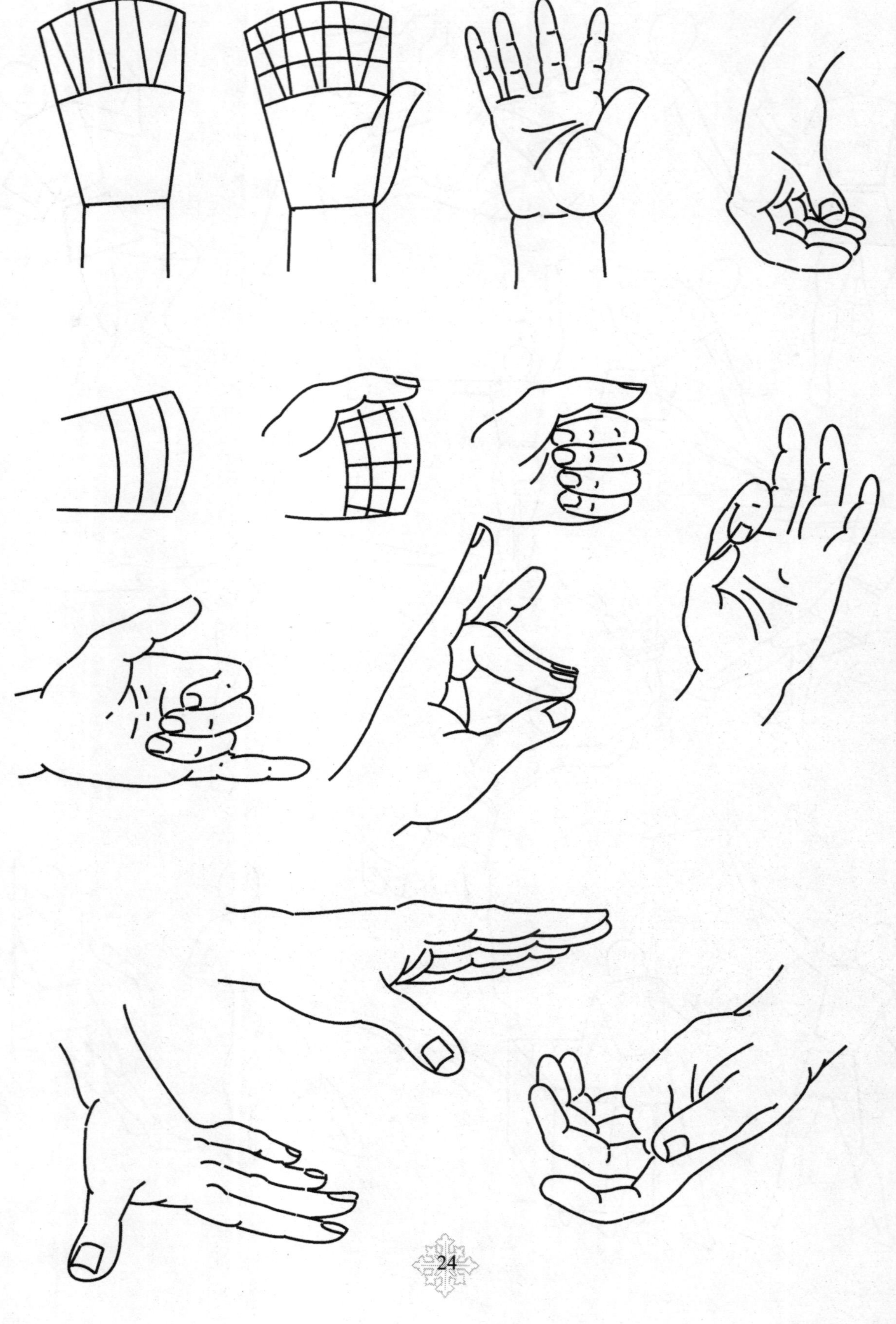

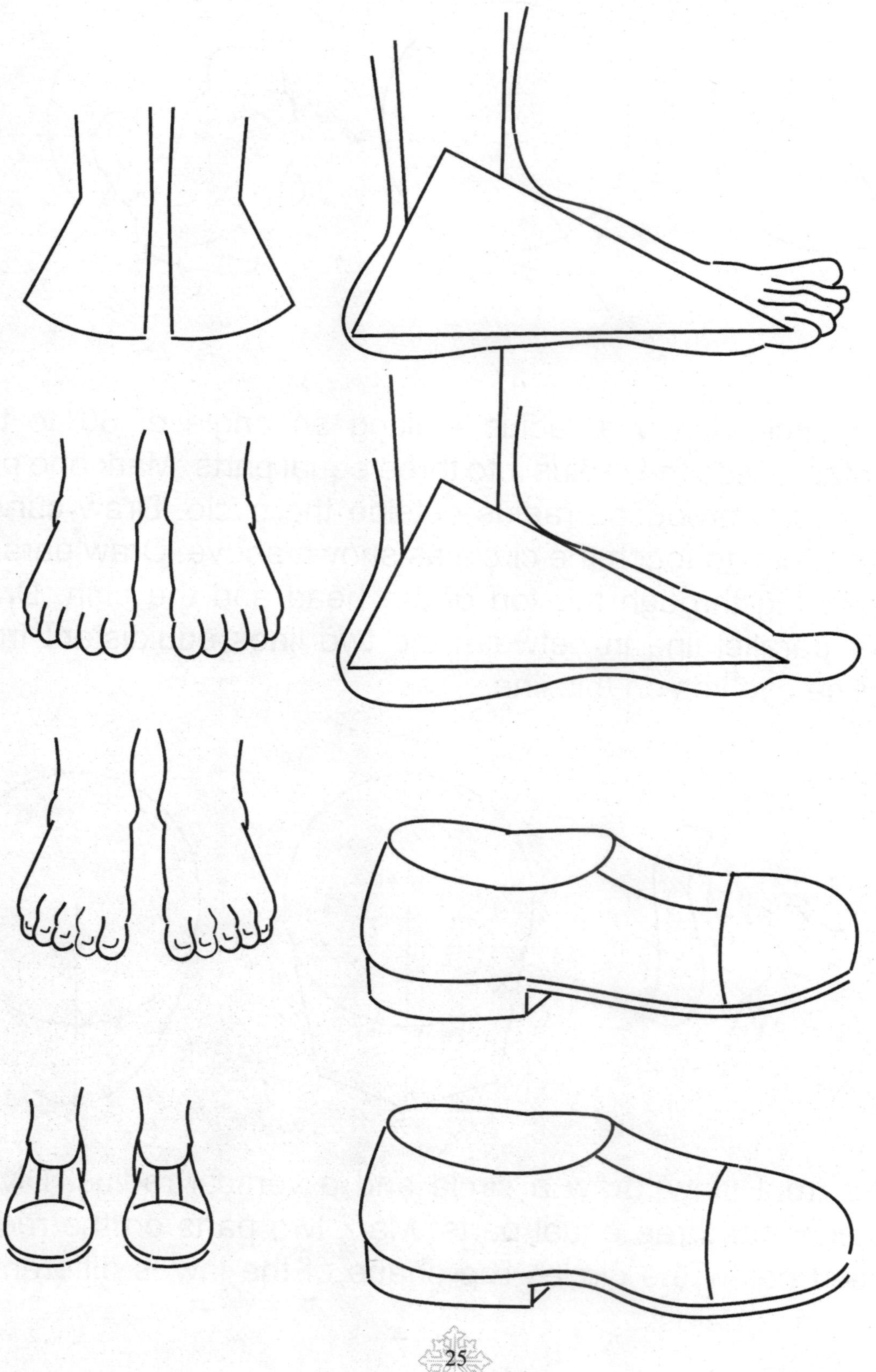

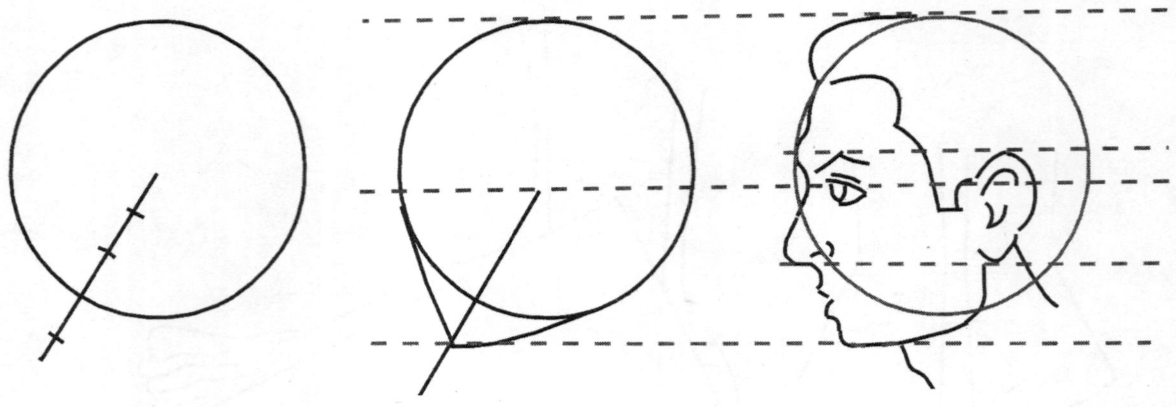

Draw a circle. Draw a radius making an angle of 60^0 to the horizontal. Divide the radius into three equal parts. Mark one part of this on the produced radius outside the circle. Draw curves from this point to touch the circle as shown above. Draw parallel lines passing through the top of the head and the chin. Draw another parallel line in between the two lines equidistant from them. The eye lies on this line.

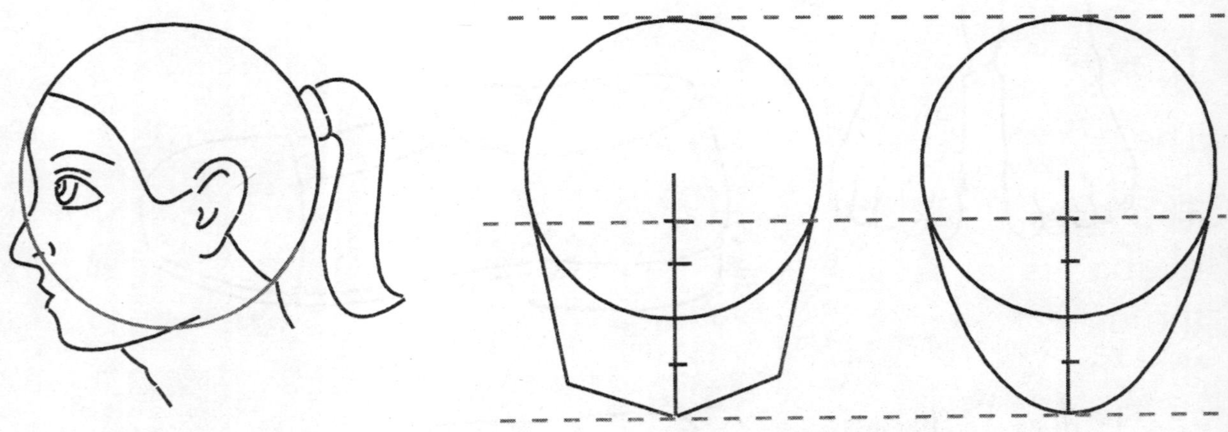

For the front view, draw a circle and a vertical radius. Divide the radius into three equal parts. Mark two parts on the radius produced below the circle. The shape of the jaw is different in males and females.

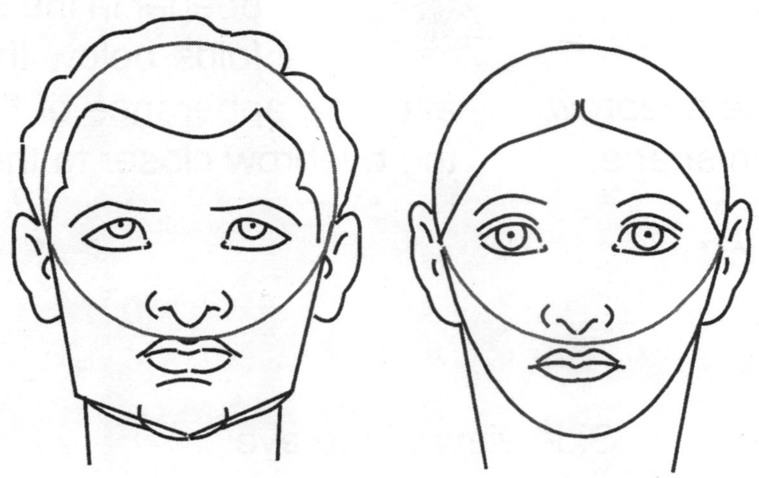

Draw two parallel lines passing through the top of the head and the chin. The eyes lie on the parallel line drawn between the two lines, equidistant from them.

The gap between the eyes is equal to the width of one eye.

The width of the nose is also the same.

The ears fit into the gap between the lines drawn through the eyebrows and the base of the nose. The mouth lies at one-third the distance between the base of the nose and the lower tip of the chin.

The female eye

The male eye

In males the eyeball is set deeper in the socket. The folds below the eyebrow alter the apperance of the eye and the eyebrow closer to the eye.

In females the eyebrow is arched in shape.

Side view of the eye

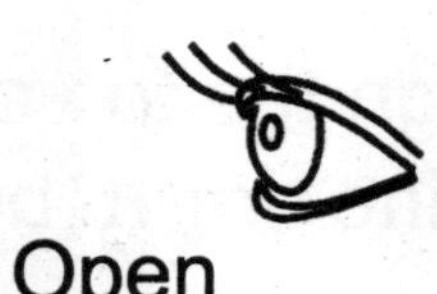

Open

Closed

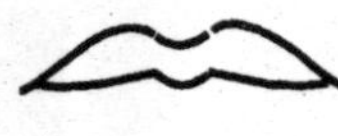

Basic apperance of lips

Simple ways to draw the nose.
A 'V' shape, two dashes and two brackets.

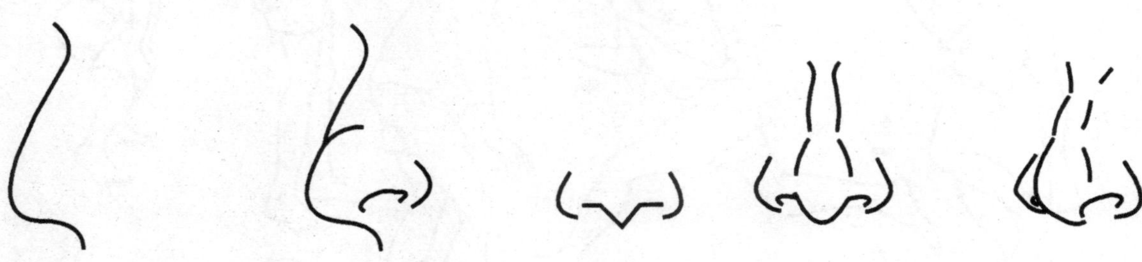

The nose and ears are the most complex to draw. They come in different shapes and sizes.

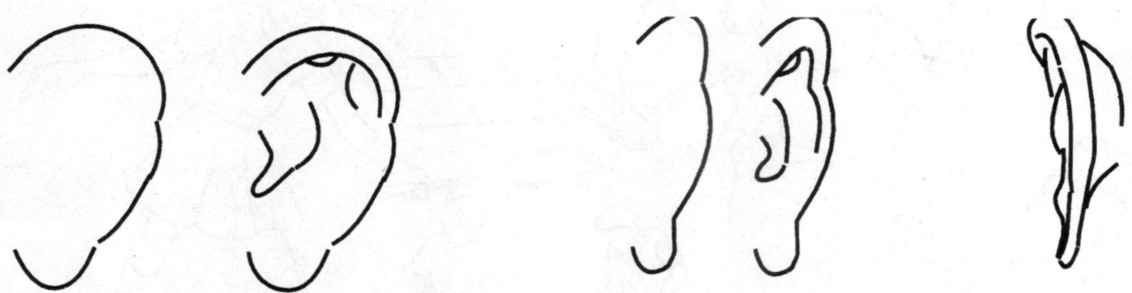

After having mastered the technique of drawing figures, it is now our turn to design characters for animated cartoon films and also learn a few facts about animation.

Nature's gift of the persistence of vision has made the cinema and tv possible. When a series of pictures with slight variations in them are shown rapidly one after another, an impression of motion is created. In the case of the cinema and tv the number of pictures shown per second is 24 and 25 respectively. The first step is to set flash or other software programmes at 25 frames per second. The usual rate in a pc is 12 frames per second.

Follow the steps shown in this book to create original cartoon characters for your graphics projects.

In animation even rigid objects take on a flexible, elastic and fluid character.

Character Designing

Most characters in animated cartoon films are based on circles, ovals and curves, which add beauty to the figures and are easy to animate.

The head, rib-cage (chest) and pelvis of all animals, including humans, are rigid. These cannot be squashed or stretched. So start with a circle for the head, one for the chest and one for the pelvis. For front view in humans they remain circles, but in side view the circle for the chest will be flattened to an ellipse.

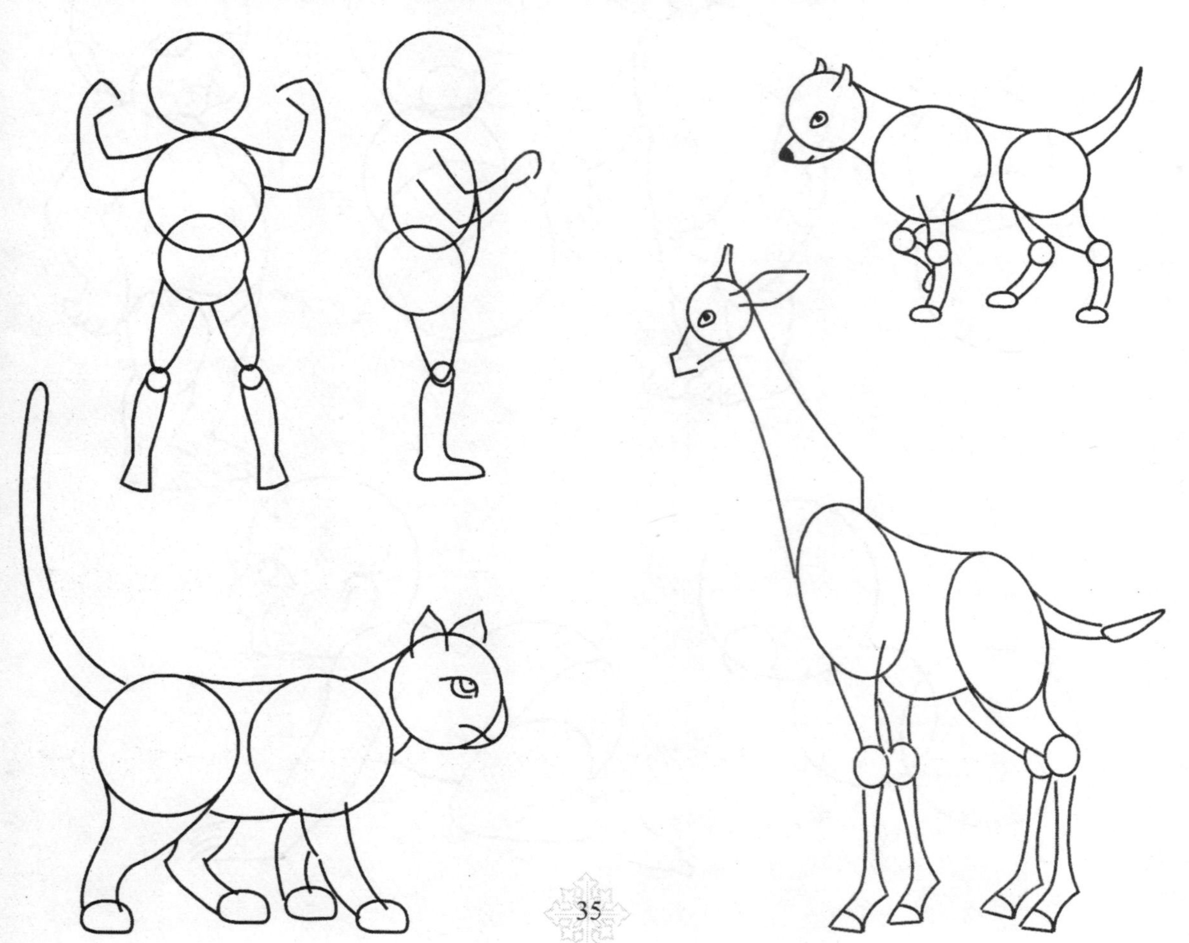

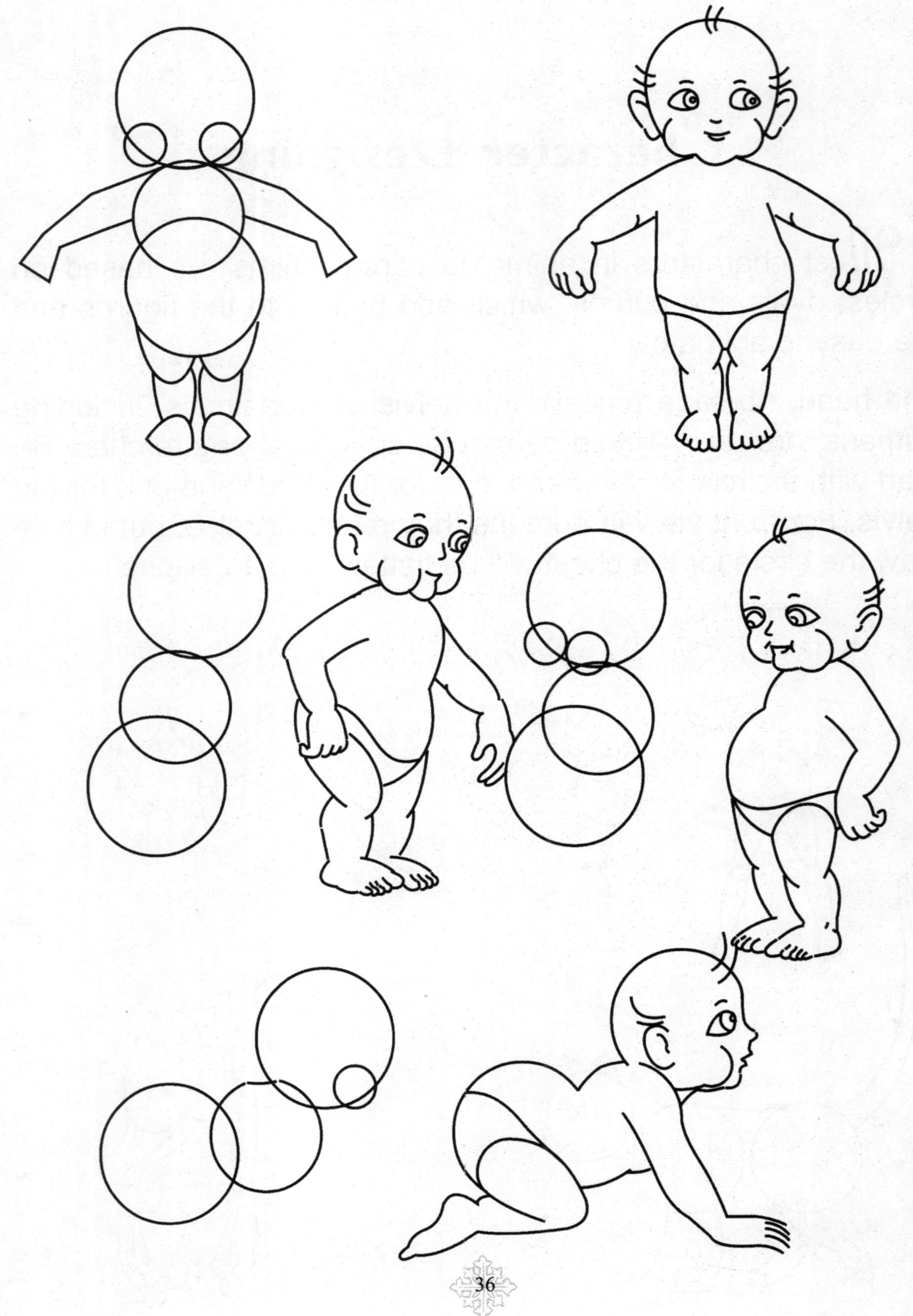

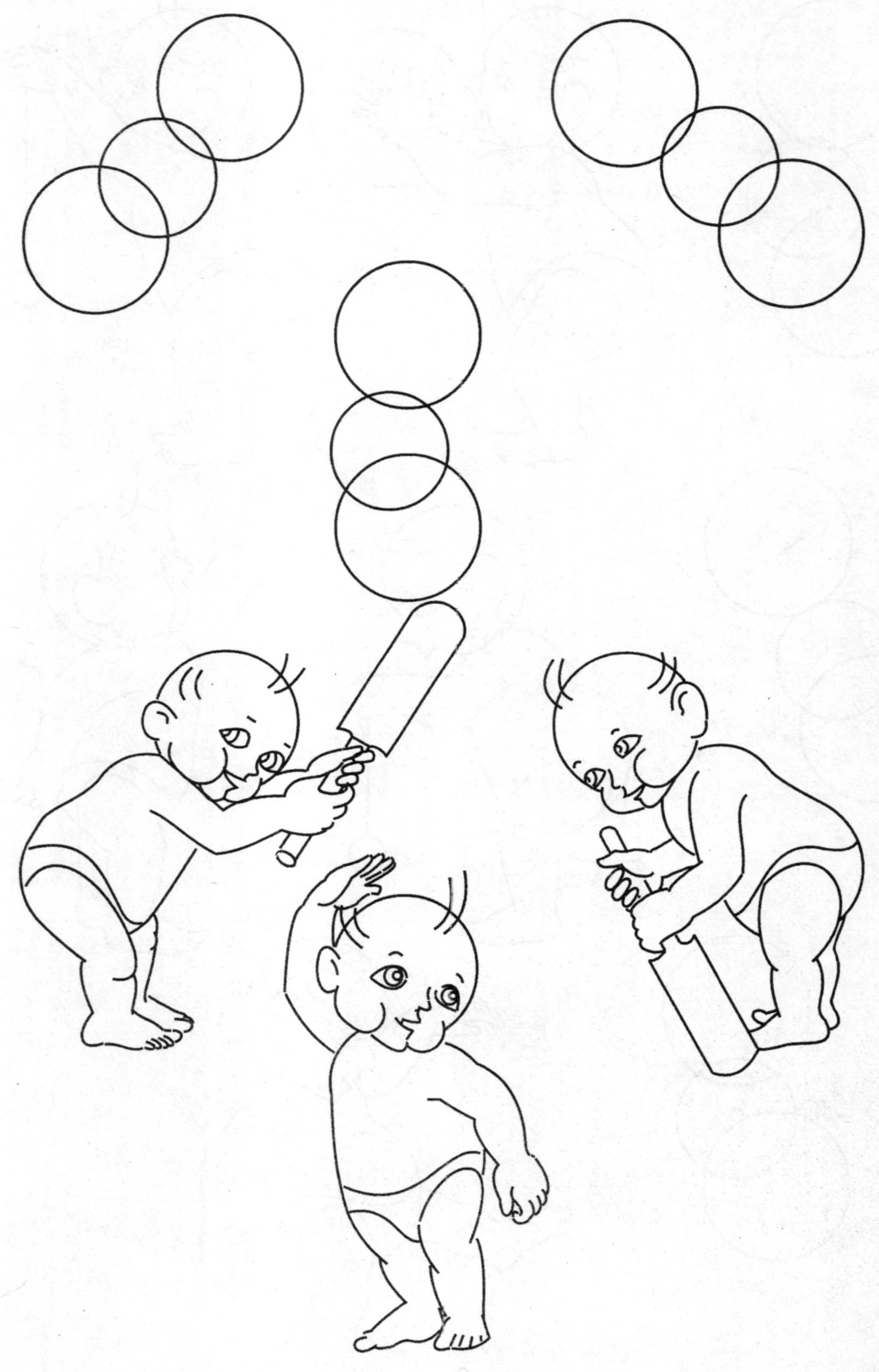

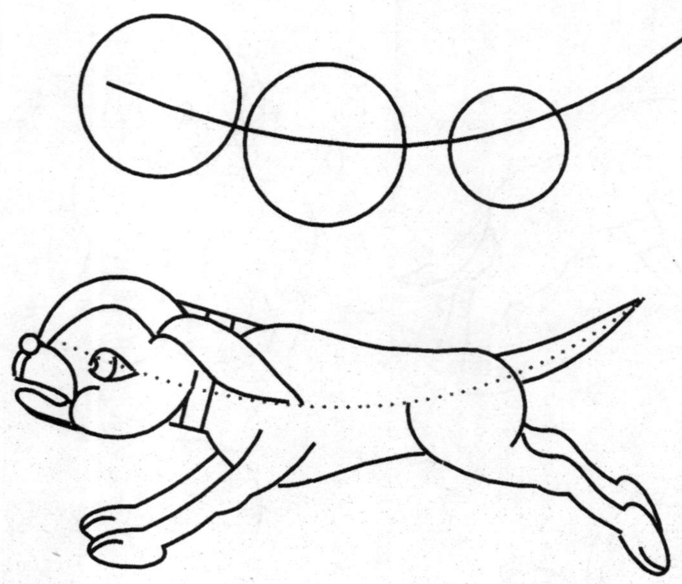

During every action, the basic elements of the figure are distributed along a smooth curved line called the line of action.

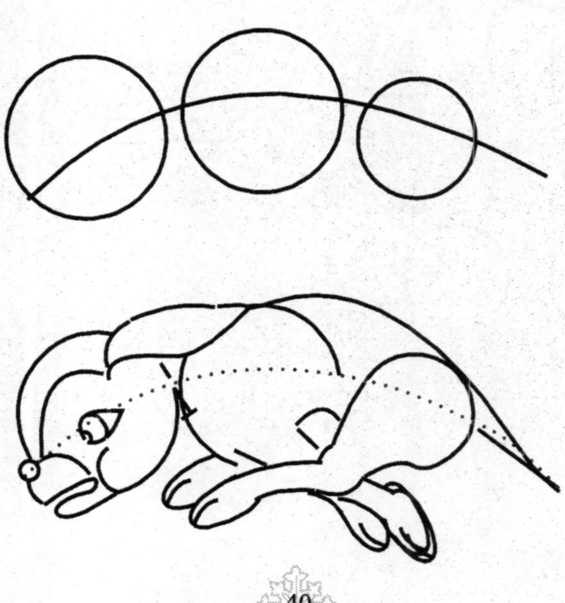

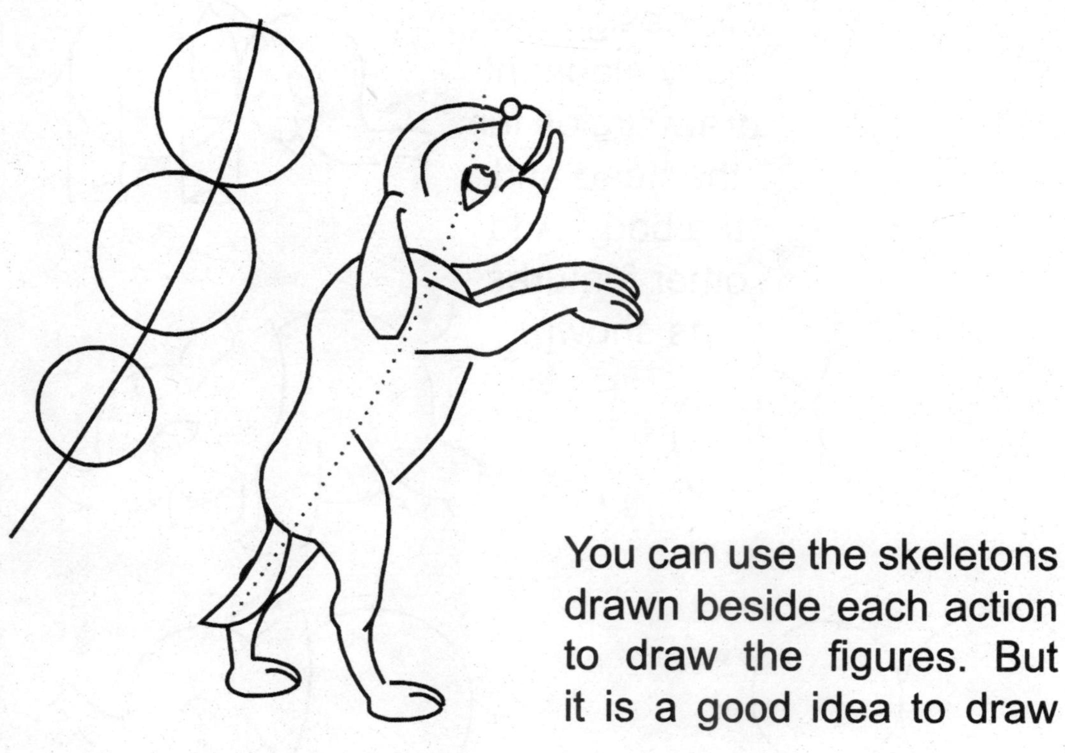

You can use the skeletons drawn beside each action to draw the figures. But it is a good idea to draw the figures several times on separate sheets of paper, just as we did to learn the alphabets.

To design the baby elephant draw circles for the head and the body. Add other features as shown.

Design the cat as shown

and assign actions
to the character.

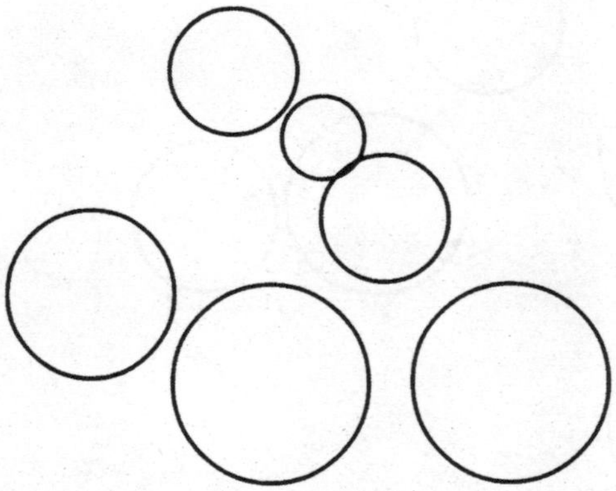

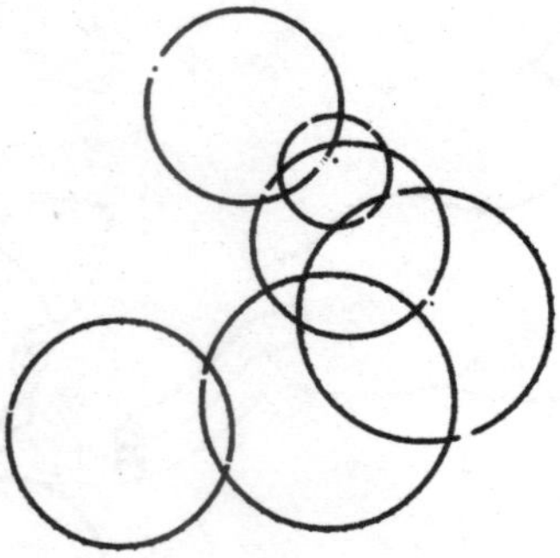

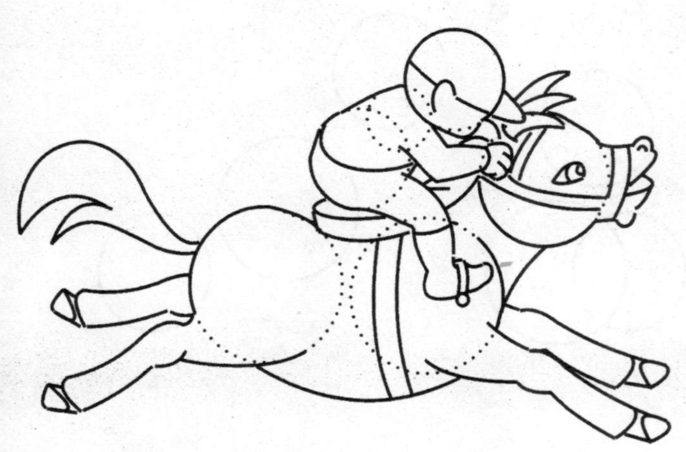

A number of circles criss-crossing may be confusing. Hence draw the horse first and then put the rider on it.

The bulls and cows in the previous pages are more on the real side. They may not allow stretching and squashing beyond a certain limit. Given below are the caricaturised version, giving ample freedom in animation.

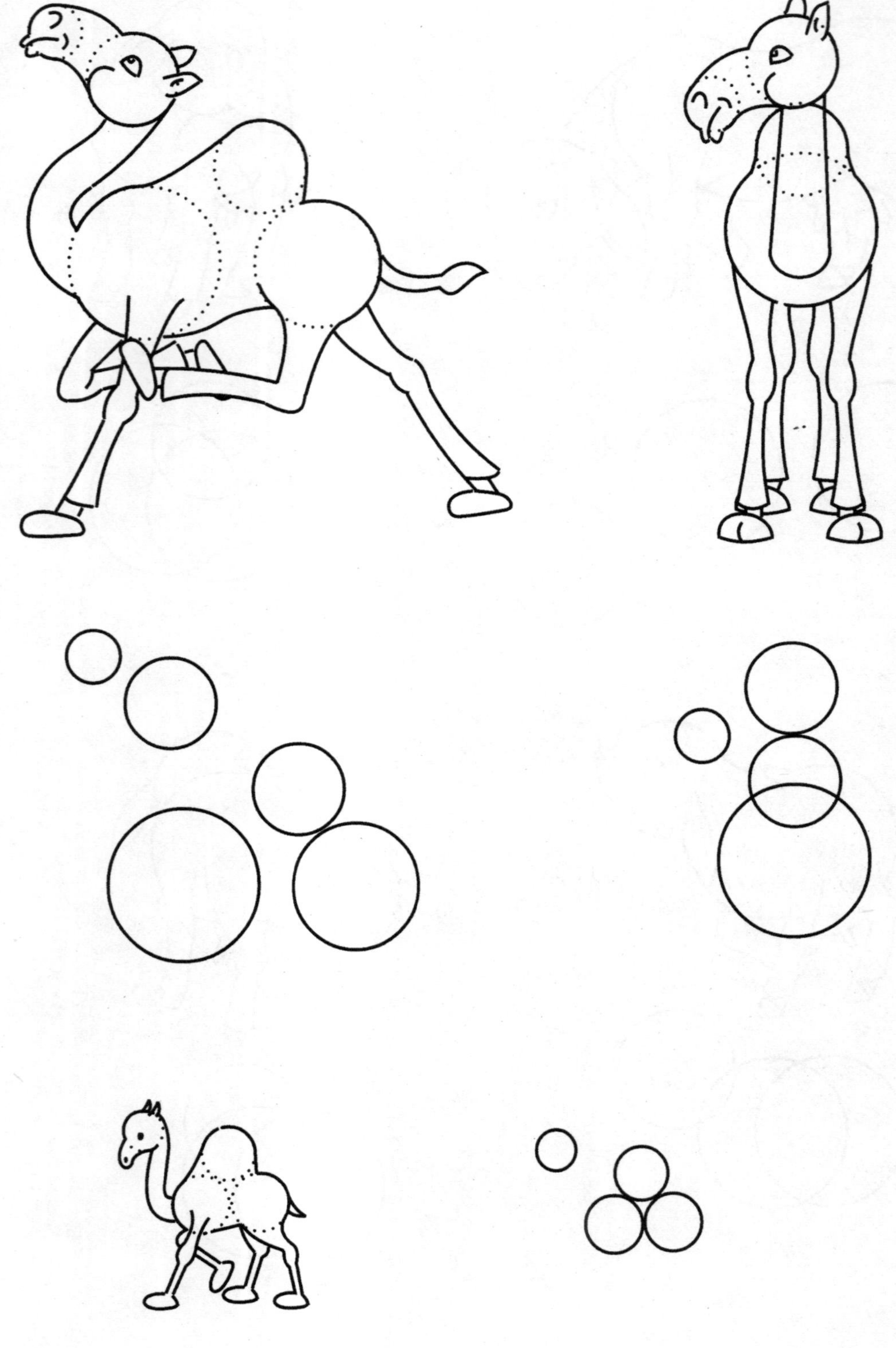

Note that the body, neck, beard and the limbs have been elongated to enhance the illusion of speed.

To draw birds, start with an egg shape for the body and a circle for the head. The egg shape is obtained by drawing tangenial curves to two circles of different sizes. The size of the head as compared with the body, varies in different species of birds.

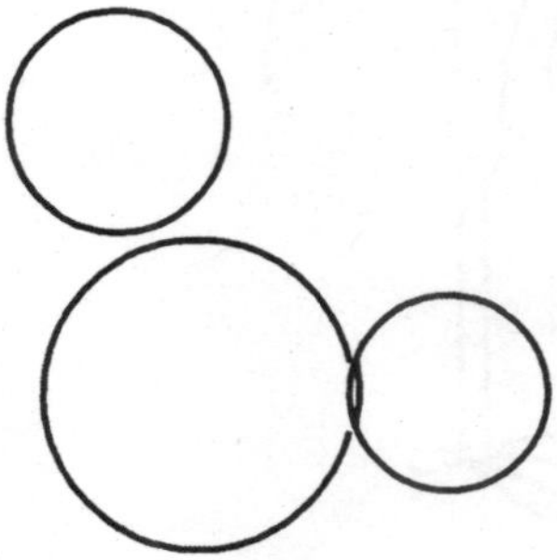

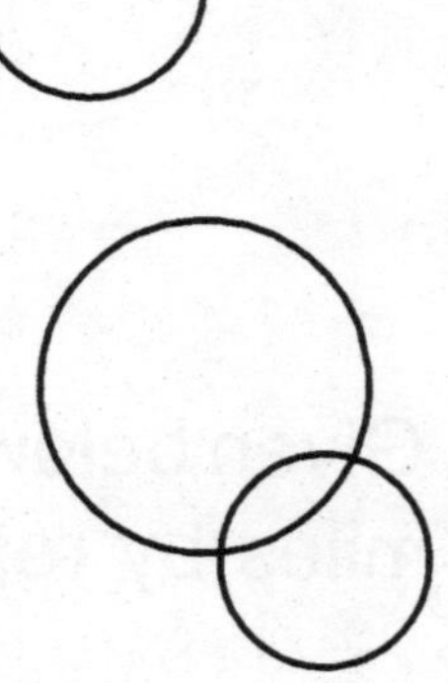

The actions of most birds are very rapid and appear to be jerky. This saves a good amount of tweening. Draw the initial position, hold for a few frames, then draw the end position and hold for a few frames (also called freeze frames).

But in flying and walking movements tweens have to be drawn.

The legs of birds bend backwards at the knee. Given below is one cycle of a step. We can make the bird walk miles by repeating the cycle.

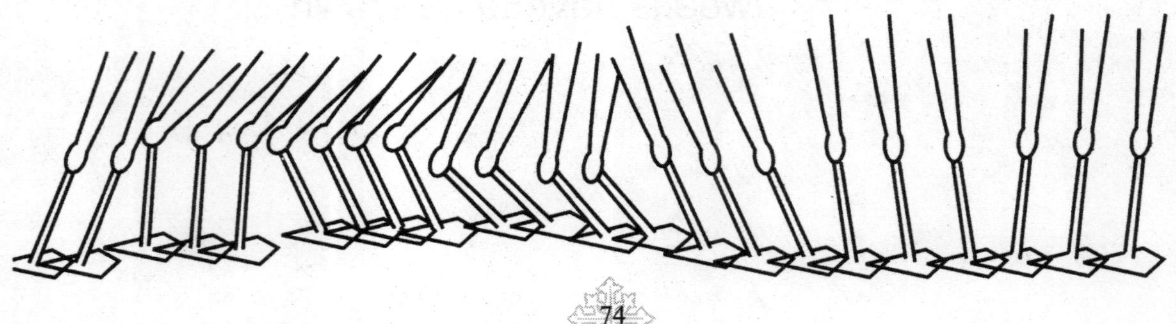

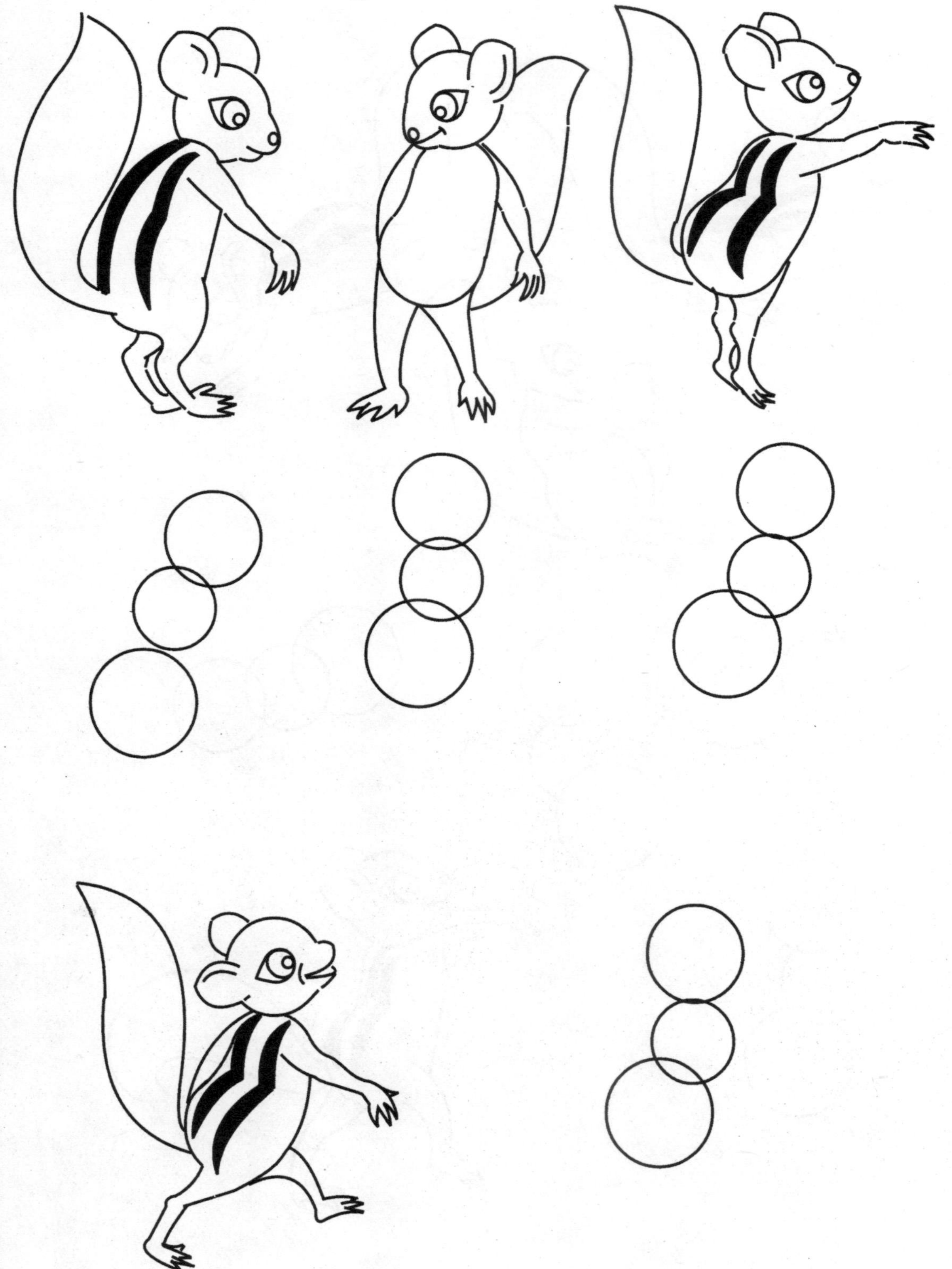

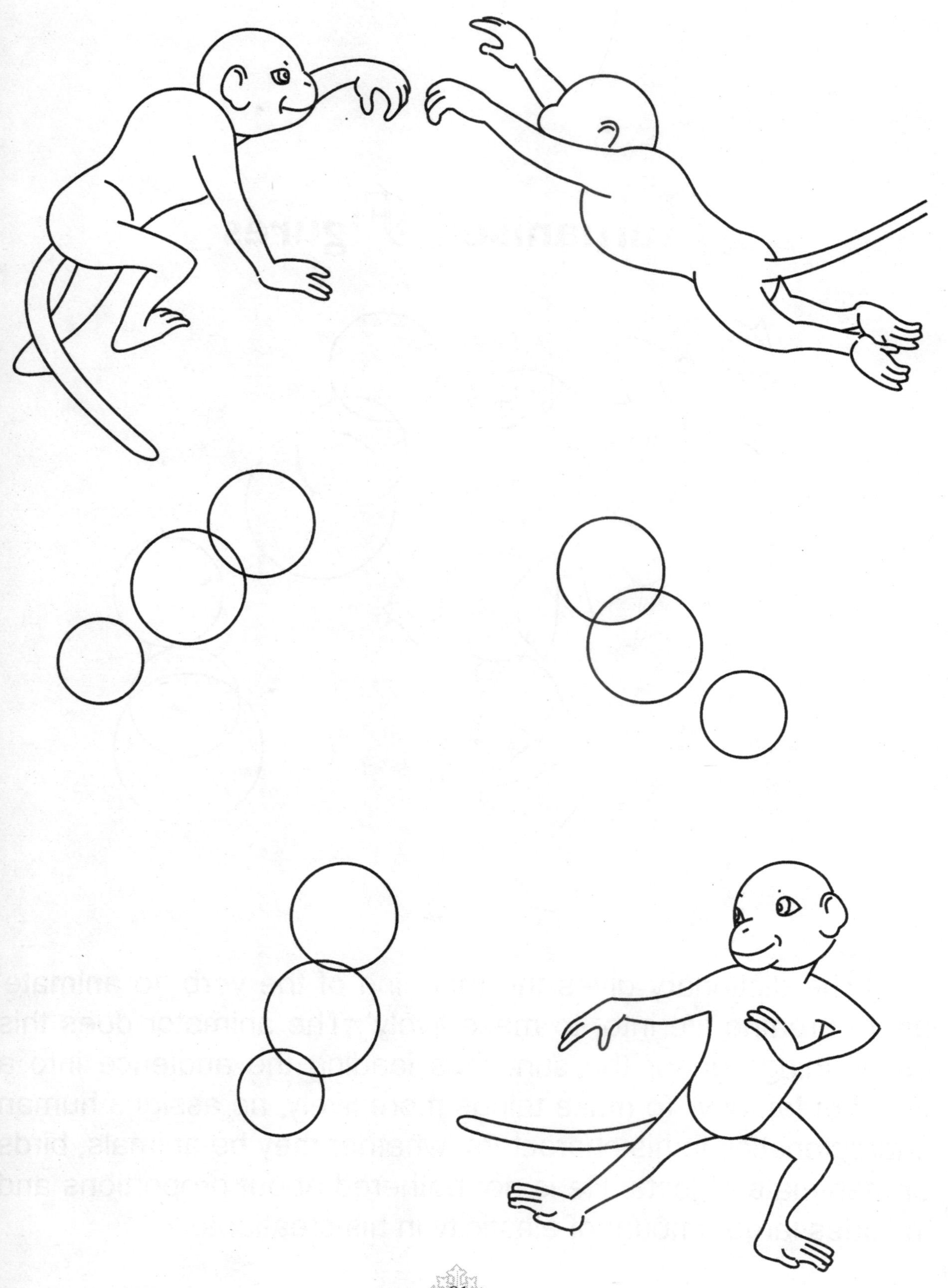

Humanised Figures

The dictionary gives the meaning of the verb 'to animate' as 'to breathe life into, to make lively'. The animator does this on all things under the sun, thus leading the audience into a world of fantasy. To make things more lively, he assigns human characteristics to his characters, whether they be animals, birds or inanimate objects. He is not bothered about proportions and includes large amount of elasticity in his creations.

Giving baby-like characteristics to the figures adds charm and more thrill to the world of fantasy.

Give your figures large eyes and girls' clothes – they become alluring females.

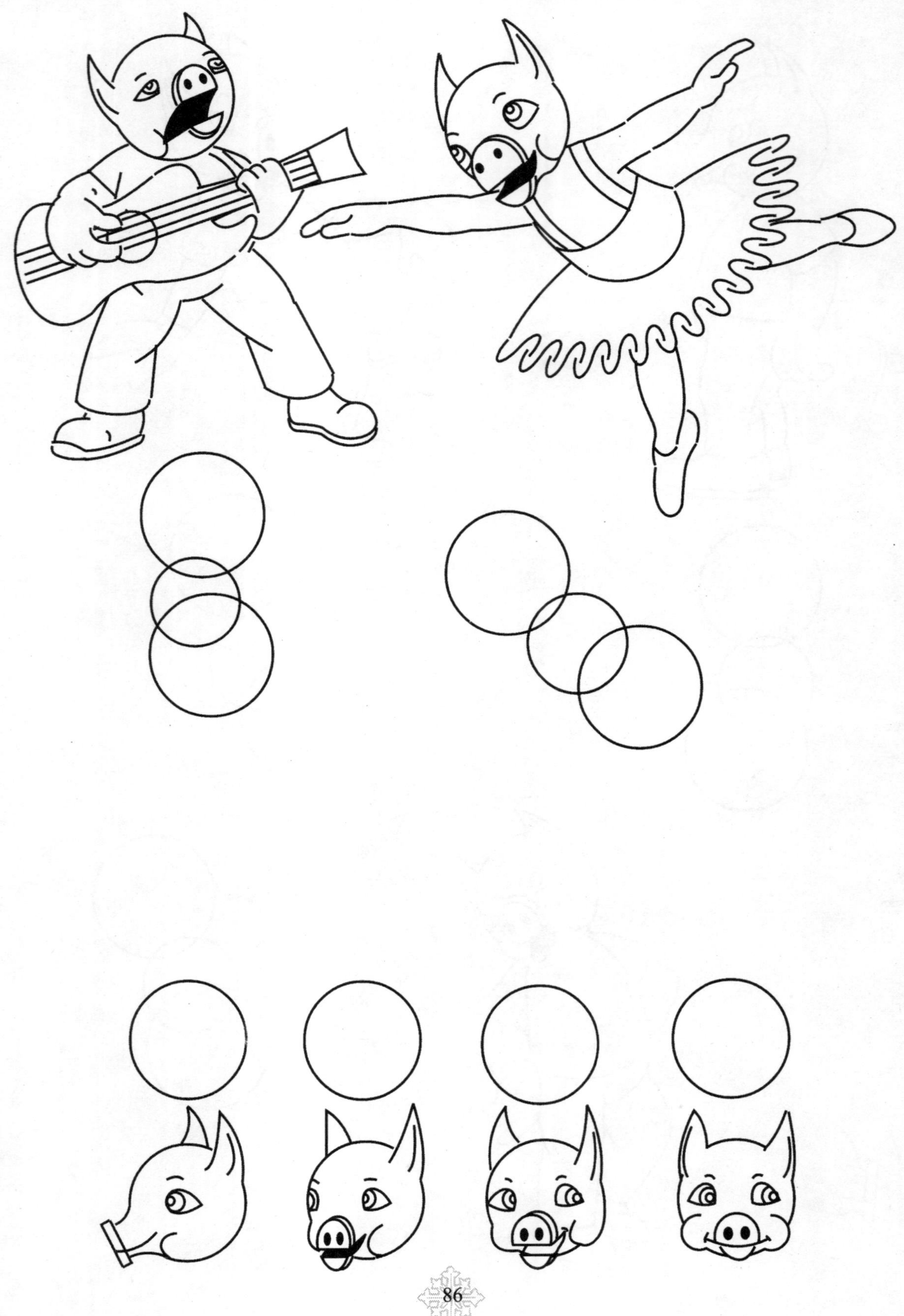

A deer is a real dear. Give it large eyes, ears and slender limbs to turn it into a charming character.

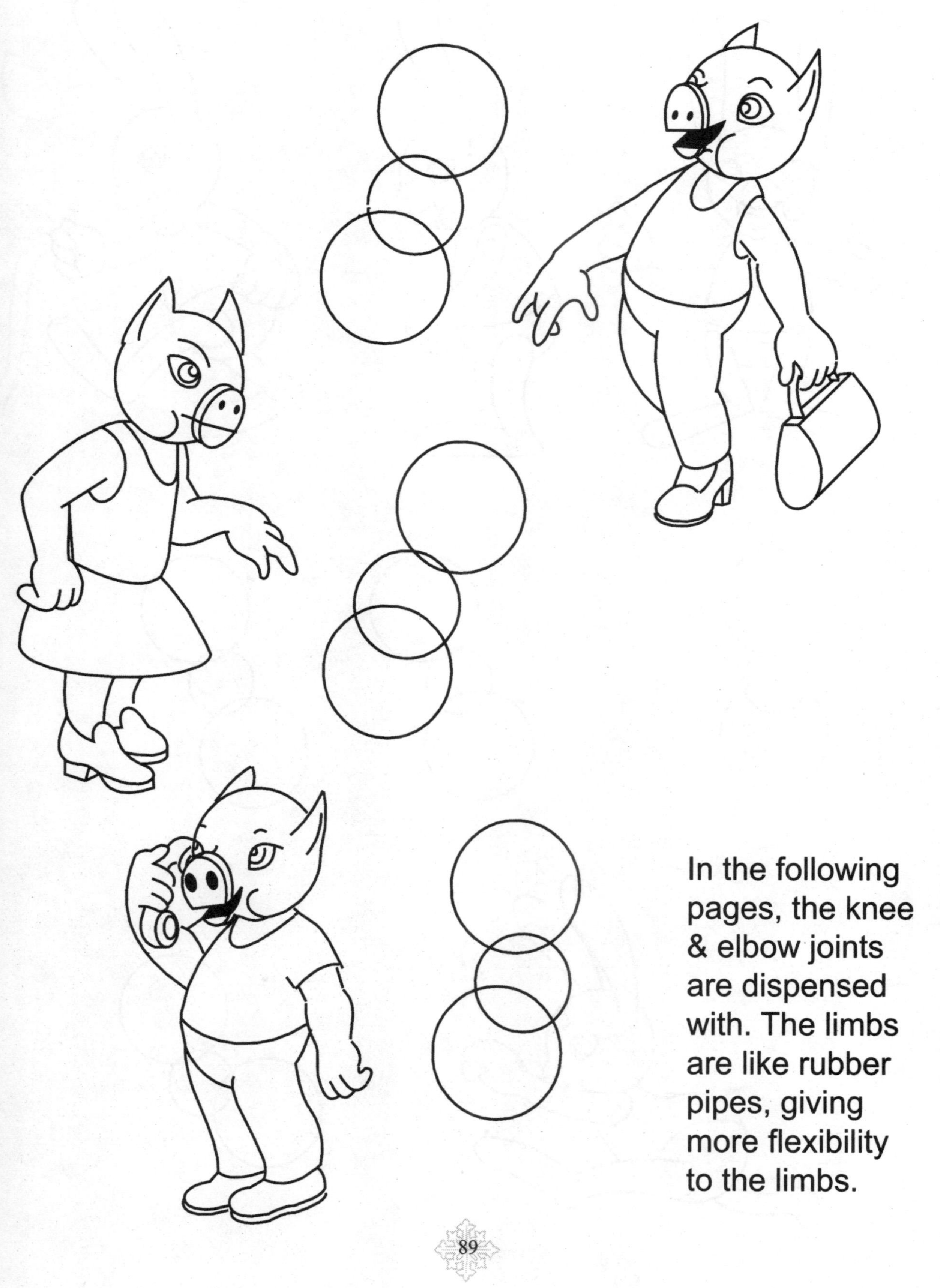

In the following pages, the knee & elbow joints are dispensed with. The limbs are like rubber pipes, giving more flexibility to the limbs.

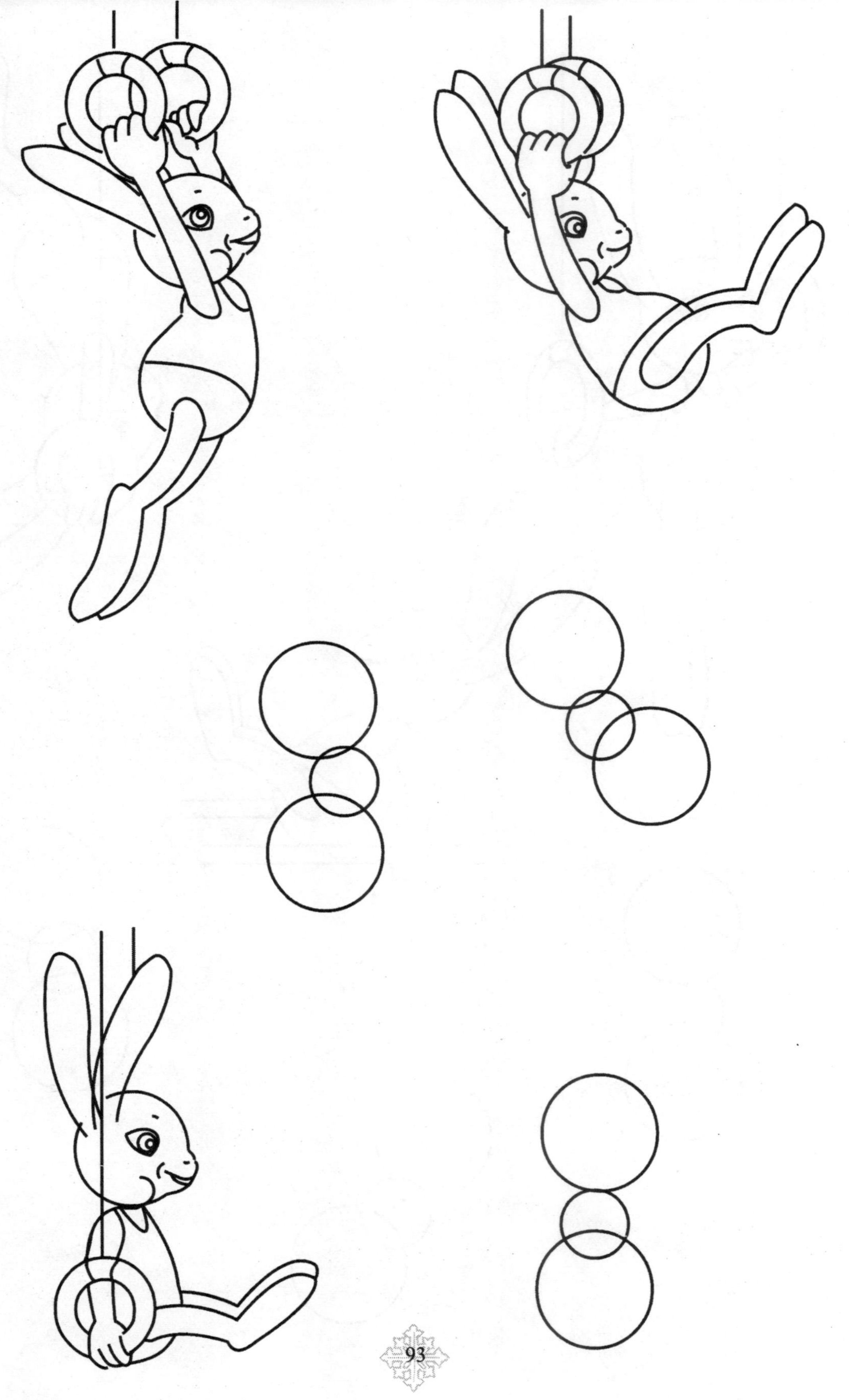

When drawing quadrupeds it is difficult to determine the comparative positions of the four legs.

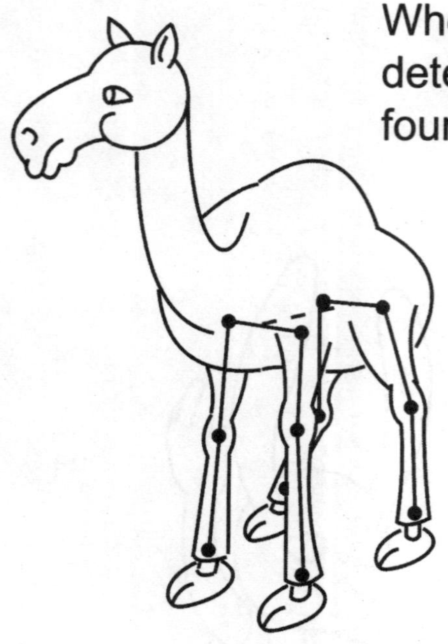

Top at eye level

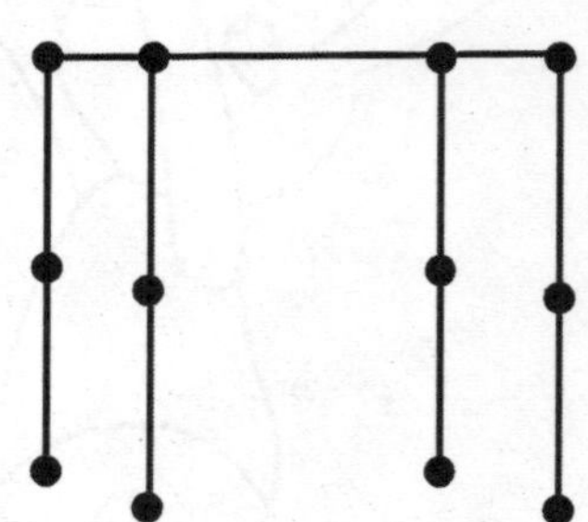

The example of a table with its top taken off will assist in this.

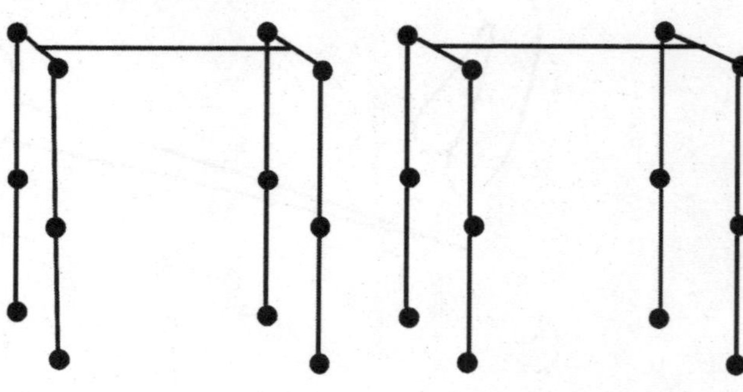

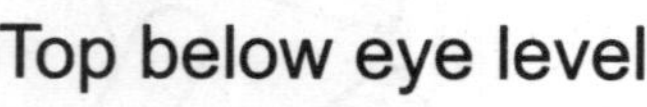

Top below eye level

In the above three examples the table is placed to the right of the viewer.

In this case, the table has moved closer to the vertical centre of the screen.

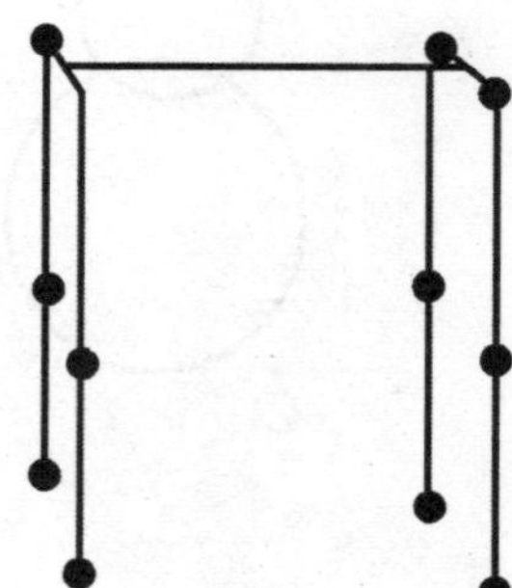

Let us observe the positions of the limbs and joints in the figures we have already drawn. Sometimes the limbs may not be seen due to their being behind the figures away from our sight. But it is useful to mark their positions in the skeletons.

The joints of both the rider and the horse.

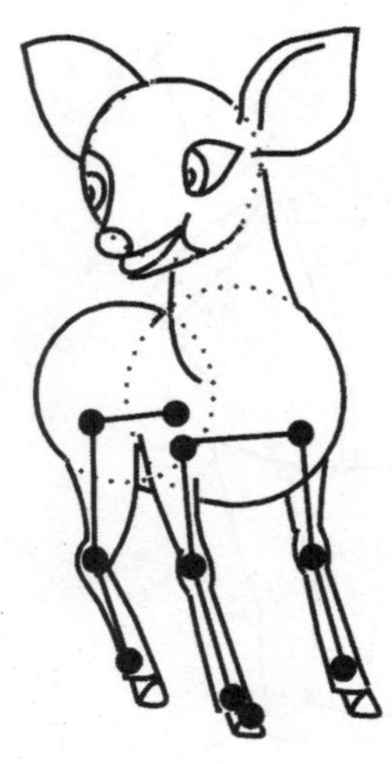

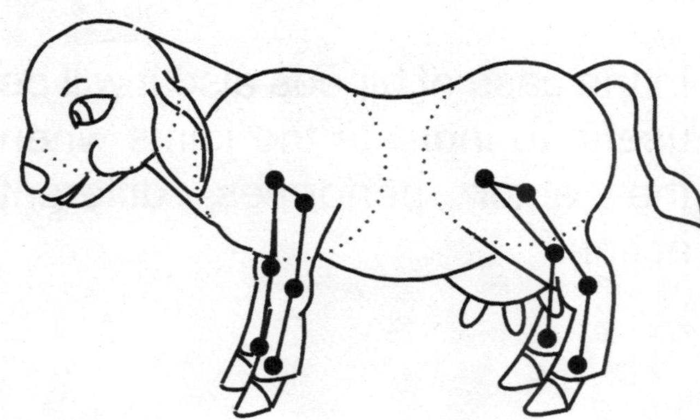

Mark the joints in the figures given below.

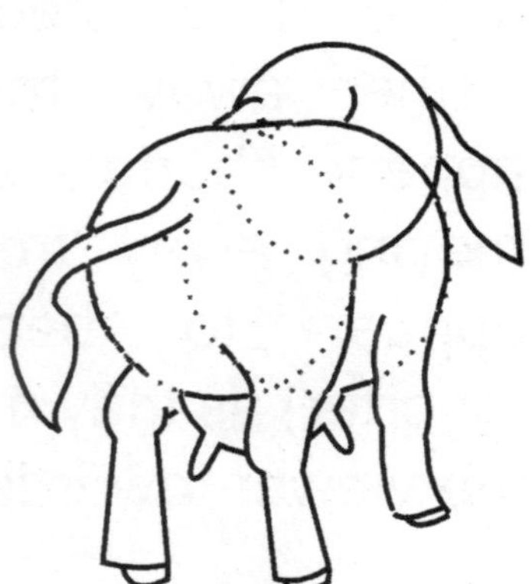

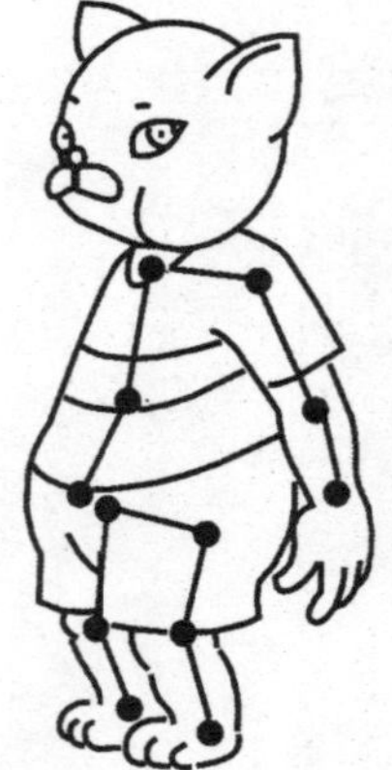

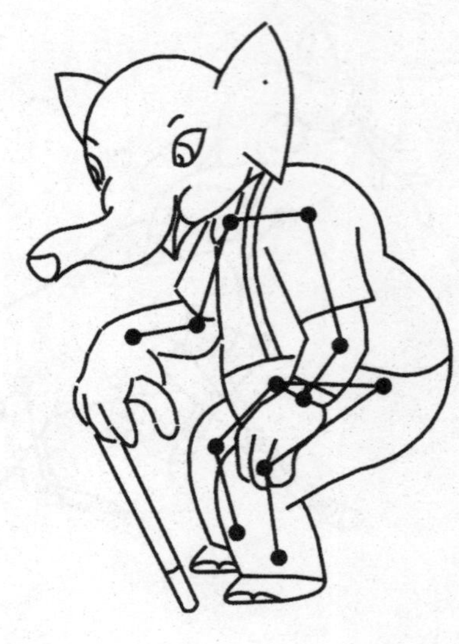

In the case of bipeds also it will be useful to indicate the joints when the actor performes different actions.

It should be noted that the limbs farther away from the viewer appear shorter, as the objects moving away from the viewer appear to become smaller (shorter) as they move away from the viewer towards the horizon.

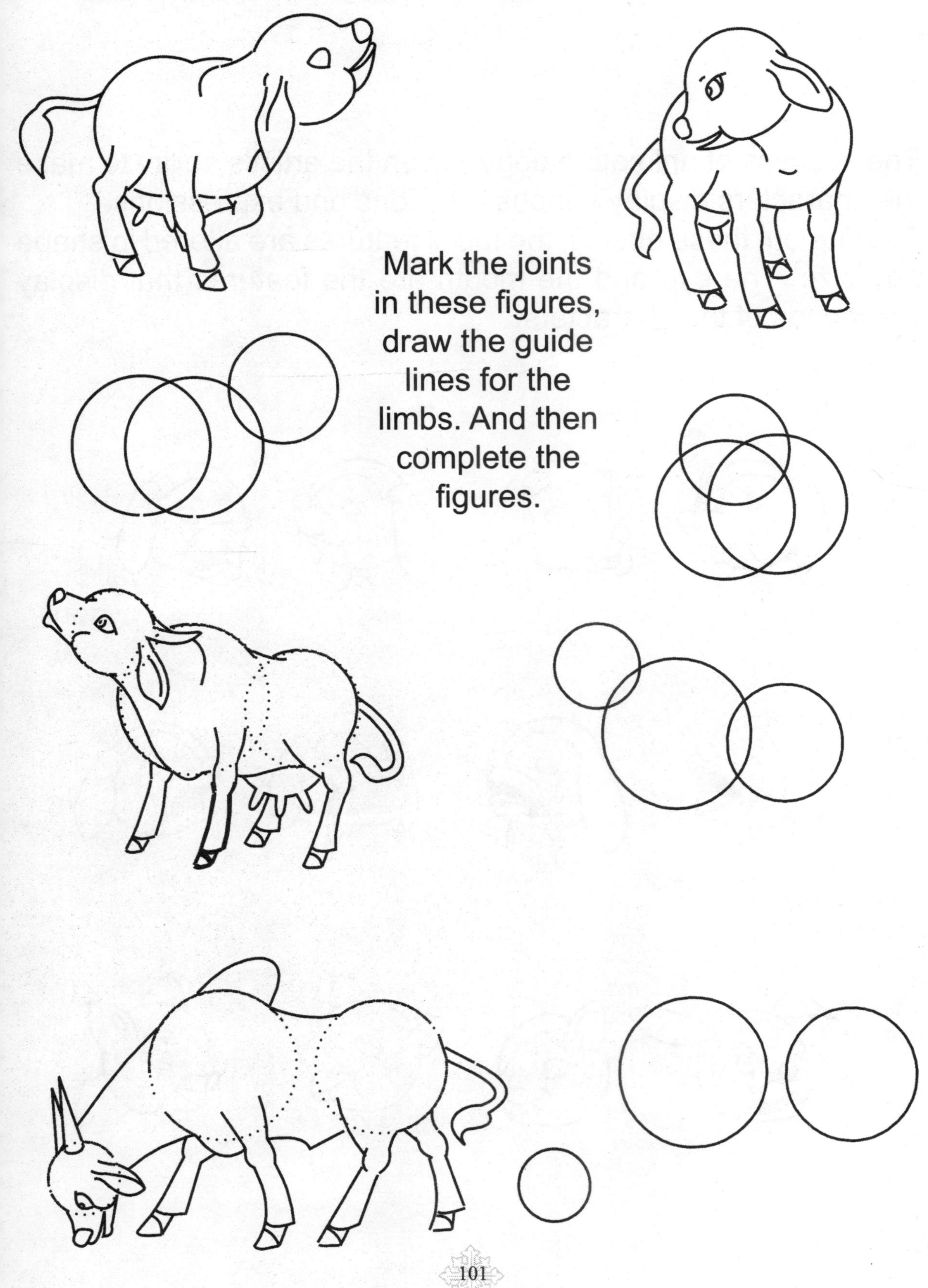
Mark the joints
in these figures,
draw the guide
lines for the
limbs. And then
complete the
figures.

The success of animation depends on the artist's ability to make the characters display various emotions and expressions.
To bring out these effects, the facial features are altered in shape and size. The eye and the mouth are the features that display the moods of the characters.

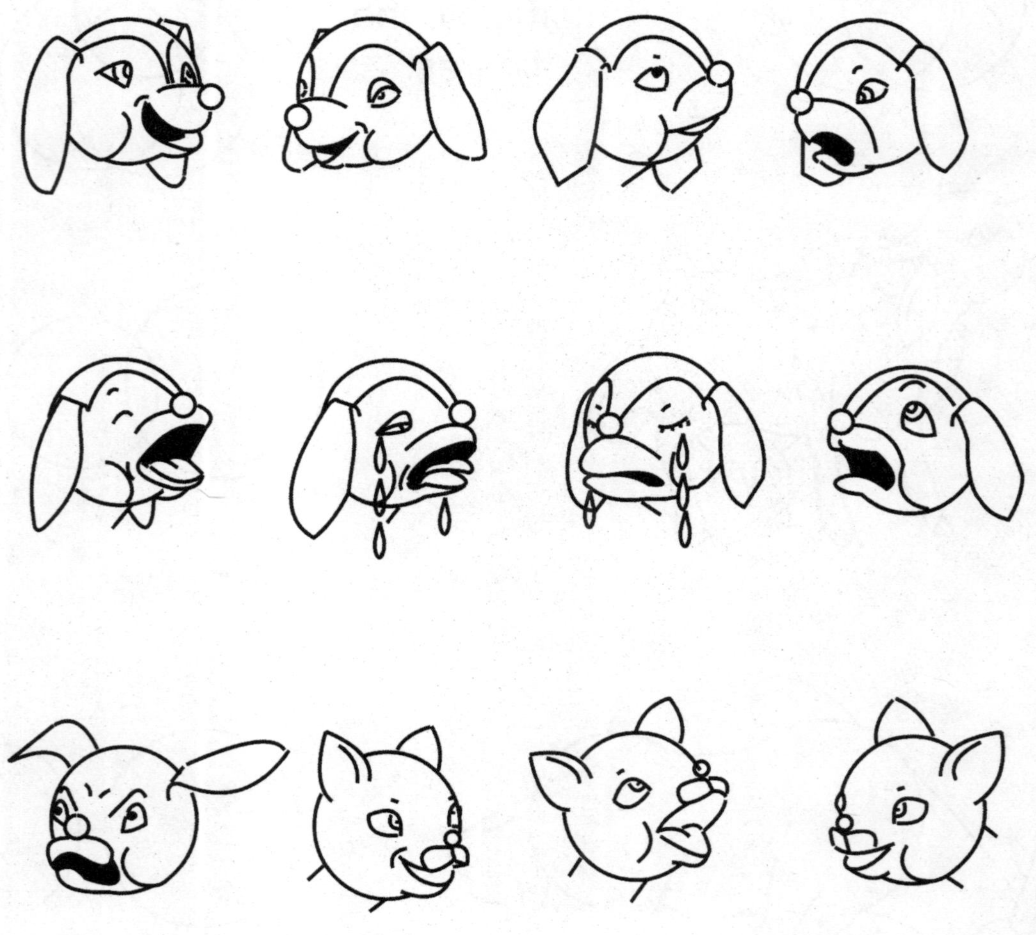

Villian of the Show

Note how the expression changes when the iris is a mere dot.

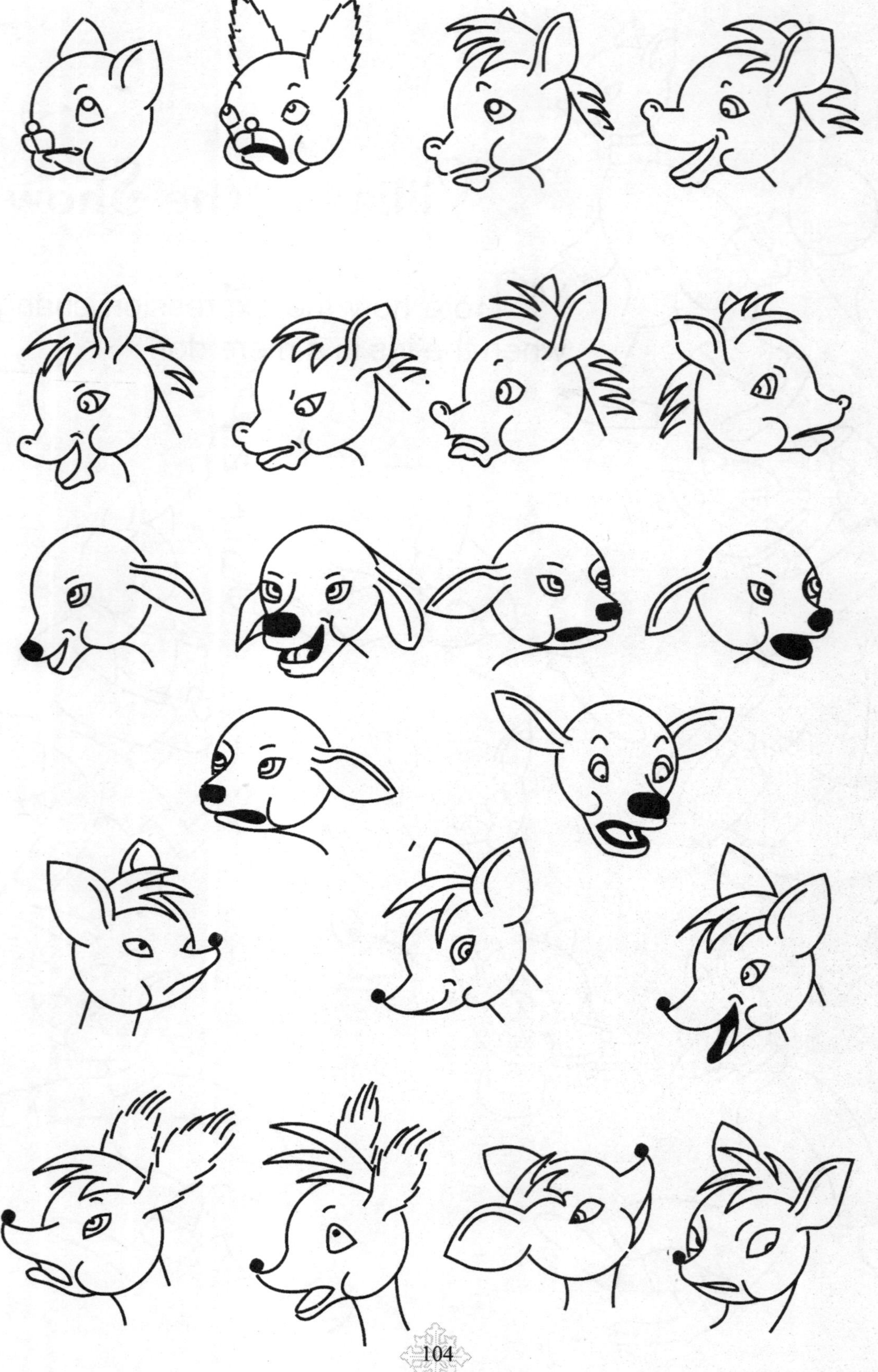

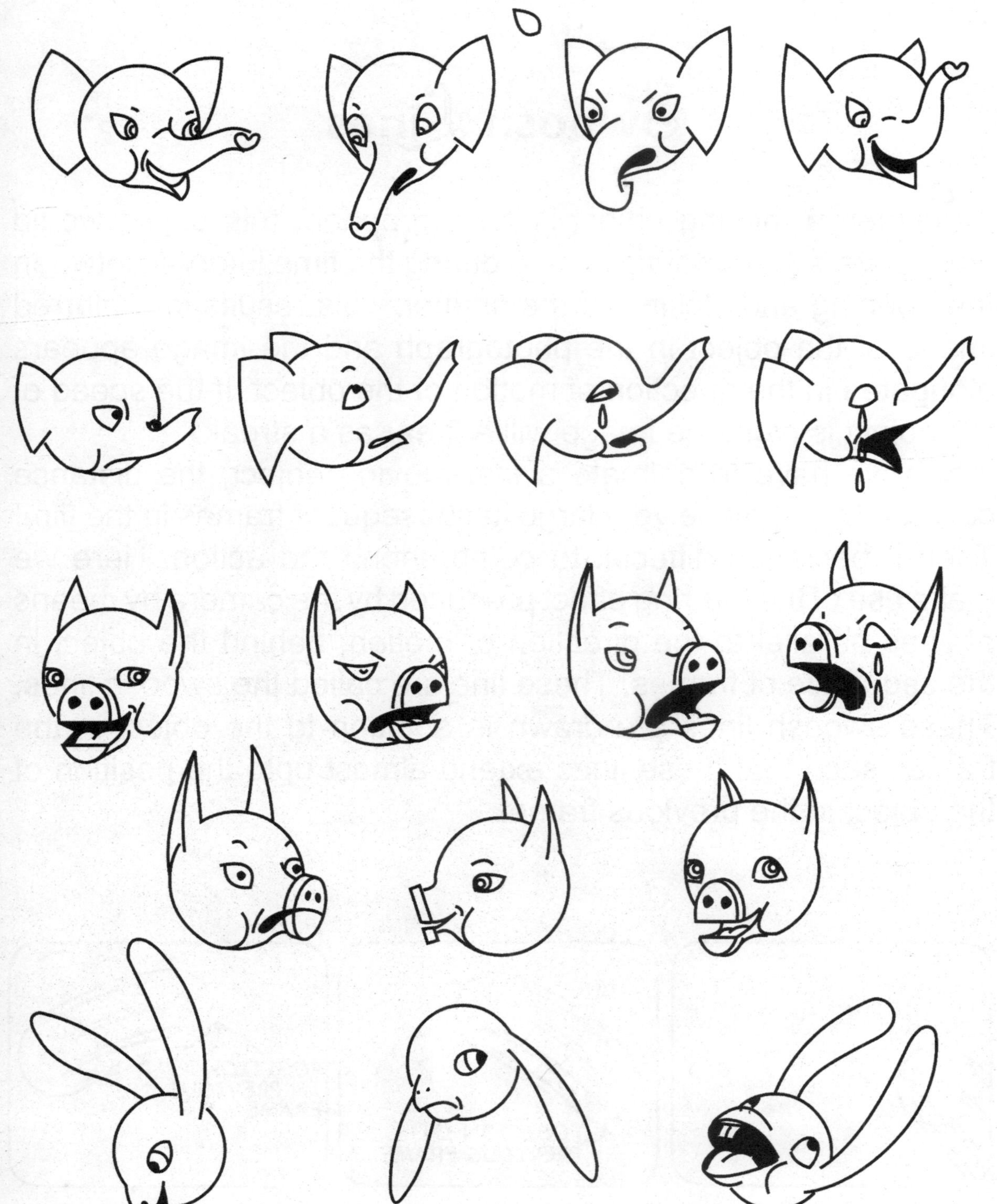

Swoosh Lines

When a moving object is photographed, this object would have covered a certain distance during the time interval between the opening and closing of the shutter. This results in a blurred image of the object in the photograph and the image appears elongated in the direction of motion of the object. If the speed of the object is high, the image will appear as a streak.

When we have to animate a fast moving object, the distance covered by it may be very large in subsequent frames in the film. Then it becomes diffucult to comprehend the action. Here we make use of the blurring effect produced by the camera by means of lines parallel to the direction of motion, behind the object in the sequence of frames. These line are called the swoosh lines. These swoosh lines are drawn in addition to the object in the frames such that these lines extend almost upto the position of the object in the previous frame.

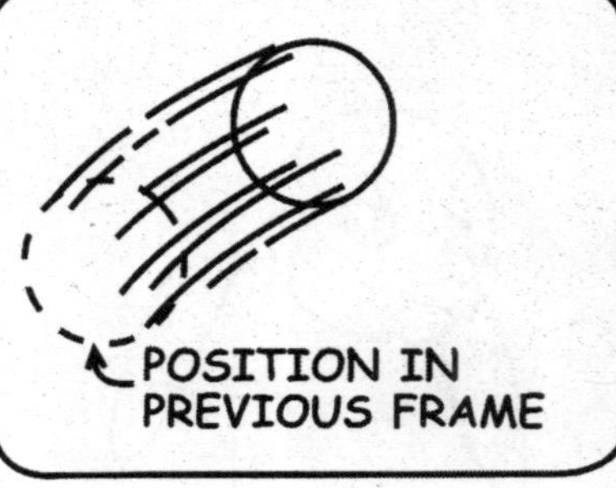

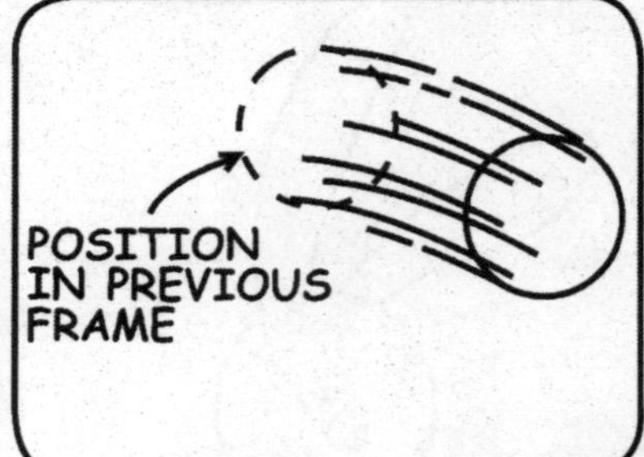

The world is full of solid objects having three dimentions – length, breadth and depth or thickness. To depict these objects in two dimentions (2D), the following points must be noted:

As objects move away from the eye they appear to become smaller in size.

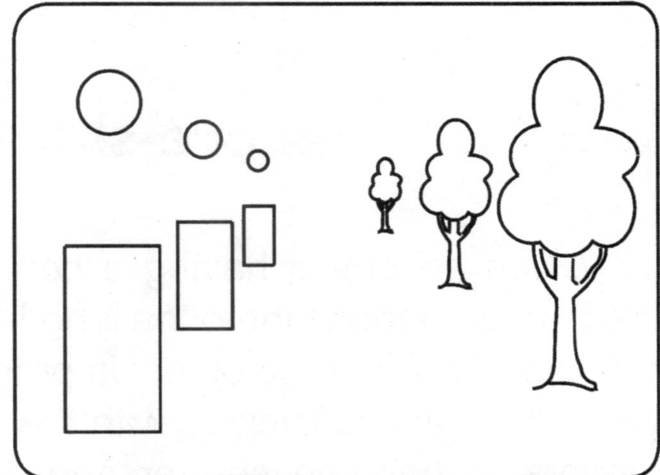

All receeding parallel lines which are perpendicular to the tv or cinema screen appear to meet at a point, which is the centre of our visual field.

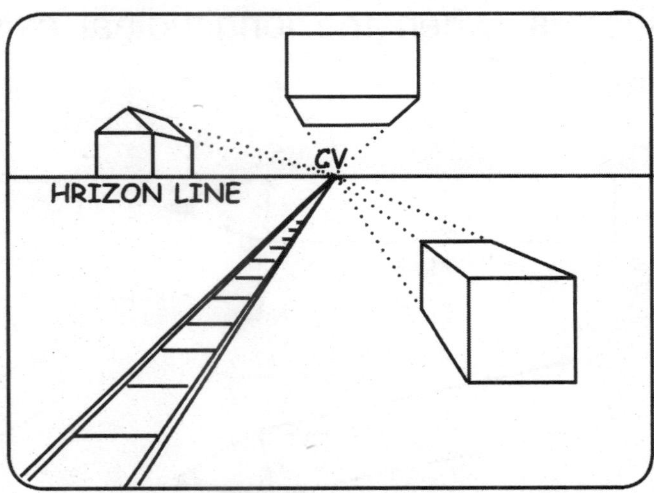

All parallel lines making an angle with the tv or cinema screen also appear to meet at points on the horizon line (hl), which is a line drawn at eye level parallel to the ground. These are called vanishing points (vp).

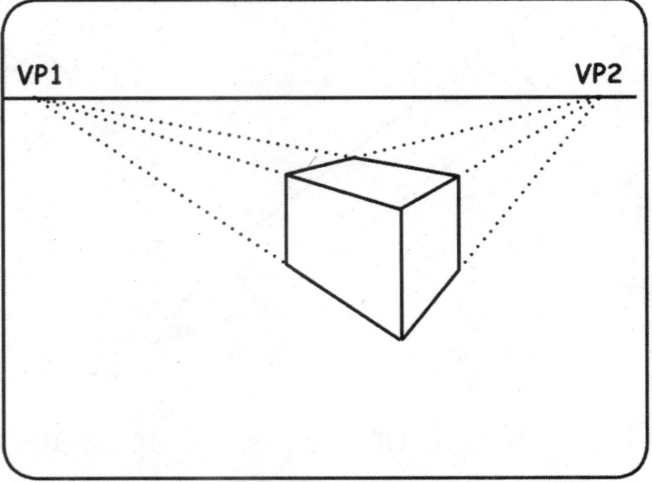

Fore-shortening

When an object having a certain length is viewed from a direction perpendicular to the length, the true length of the object is displayed. But if the object is progressively turned so that the longitudinal axis coincides with the direction of sight, the length appears to become shorter and shorter. The length appears shortest when the longitudinal axis coincides with the line of sight.

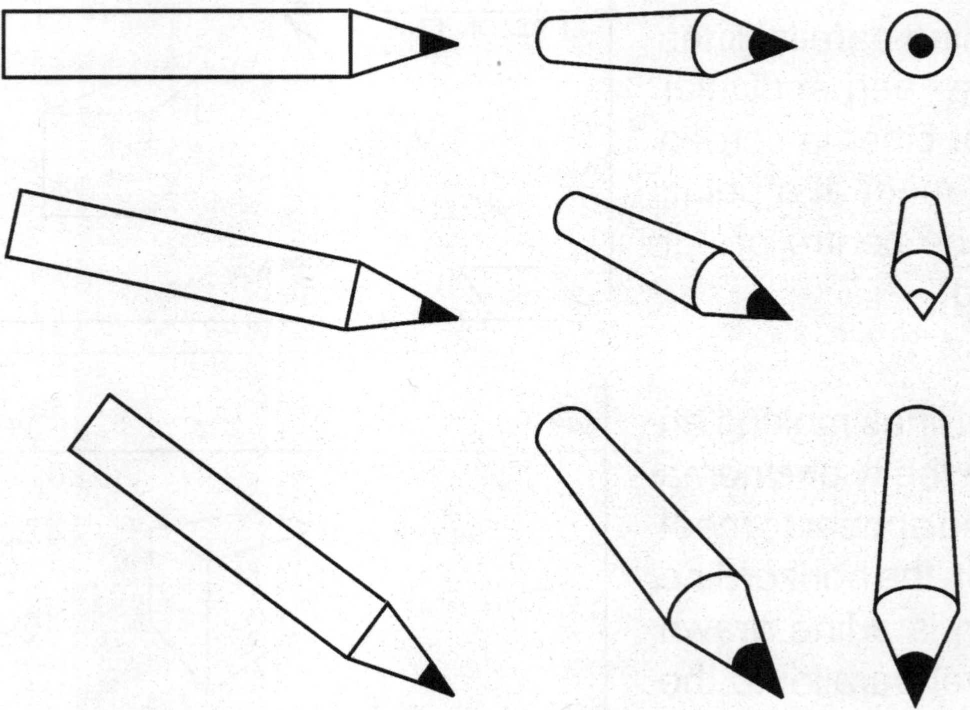

The rear end of the pencil appears narrower as it is farther away from the viewer.

Elasticity in Animation

Animation deals with objects in motion. Hence all principles in physics are applicable to them. To show more dramatic effects these principles are applied with exaggeration. Take the case of a static object which stays put due to inertia. When a force is applied to move it, the portion where the force is applied moves first, the rest of the body follows. In animation all objects are depicted to be elastic, flexible and pliable.

See how the motion of the wagon is animated below:

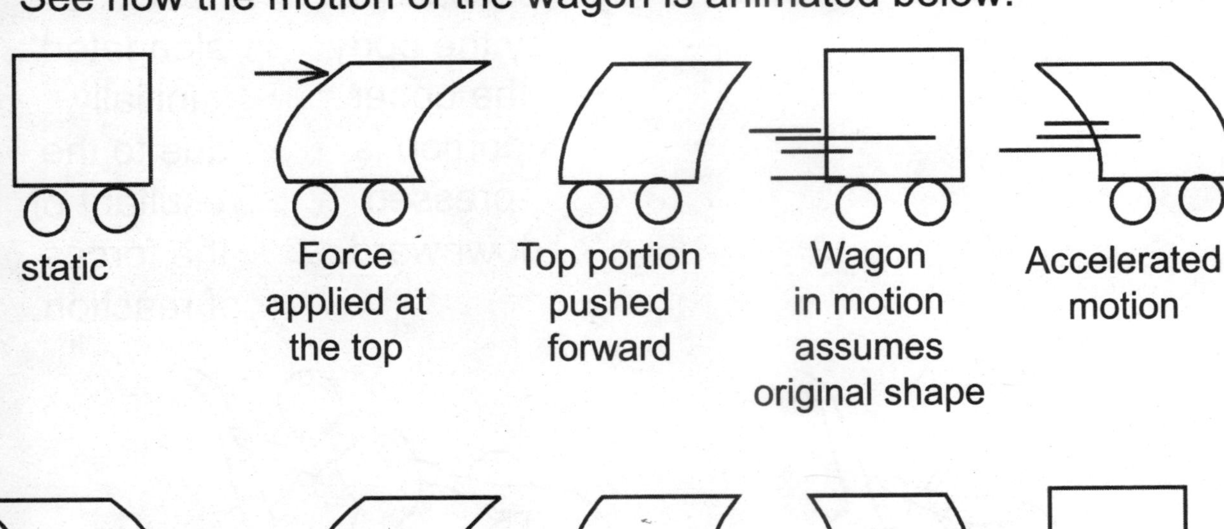

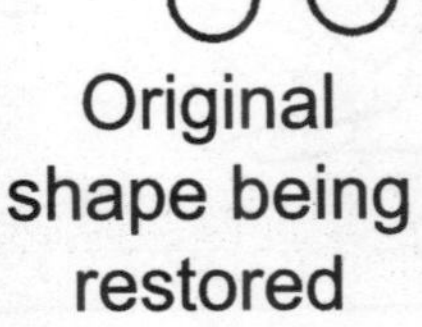
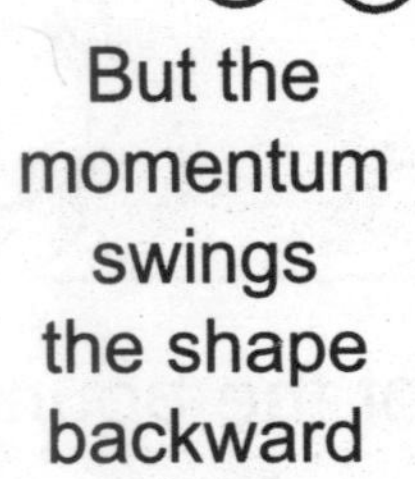
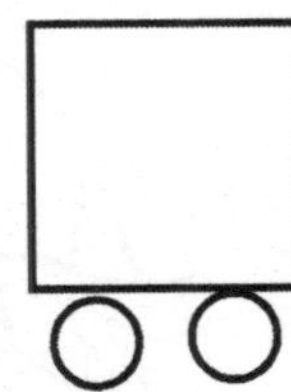

Physics of the Bouncing Ball

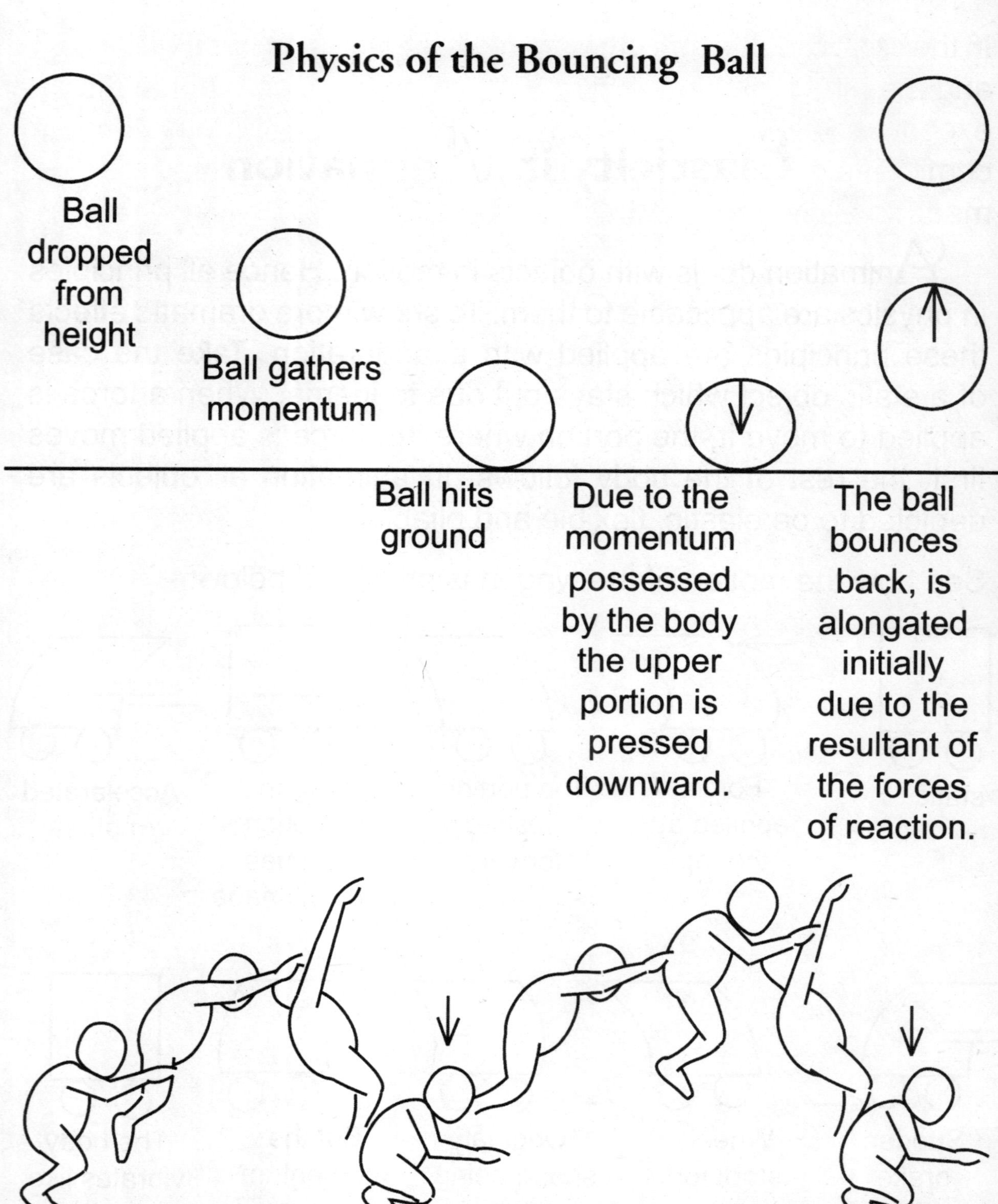

The principle of the bouncing ball holds good for all objects.

In the case of cattle and other animals the forelegs bend backward and the hind legs bend forward at the knees. The elephant is an exception, all its legs bending backward at the knees. But for comic effect both the front and back legs of all animals can be made to bend backward at the knees.

The Hind Leg

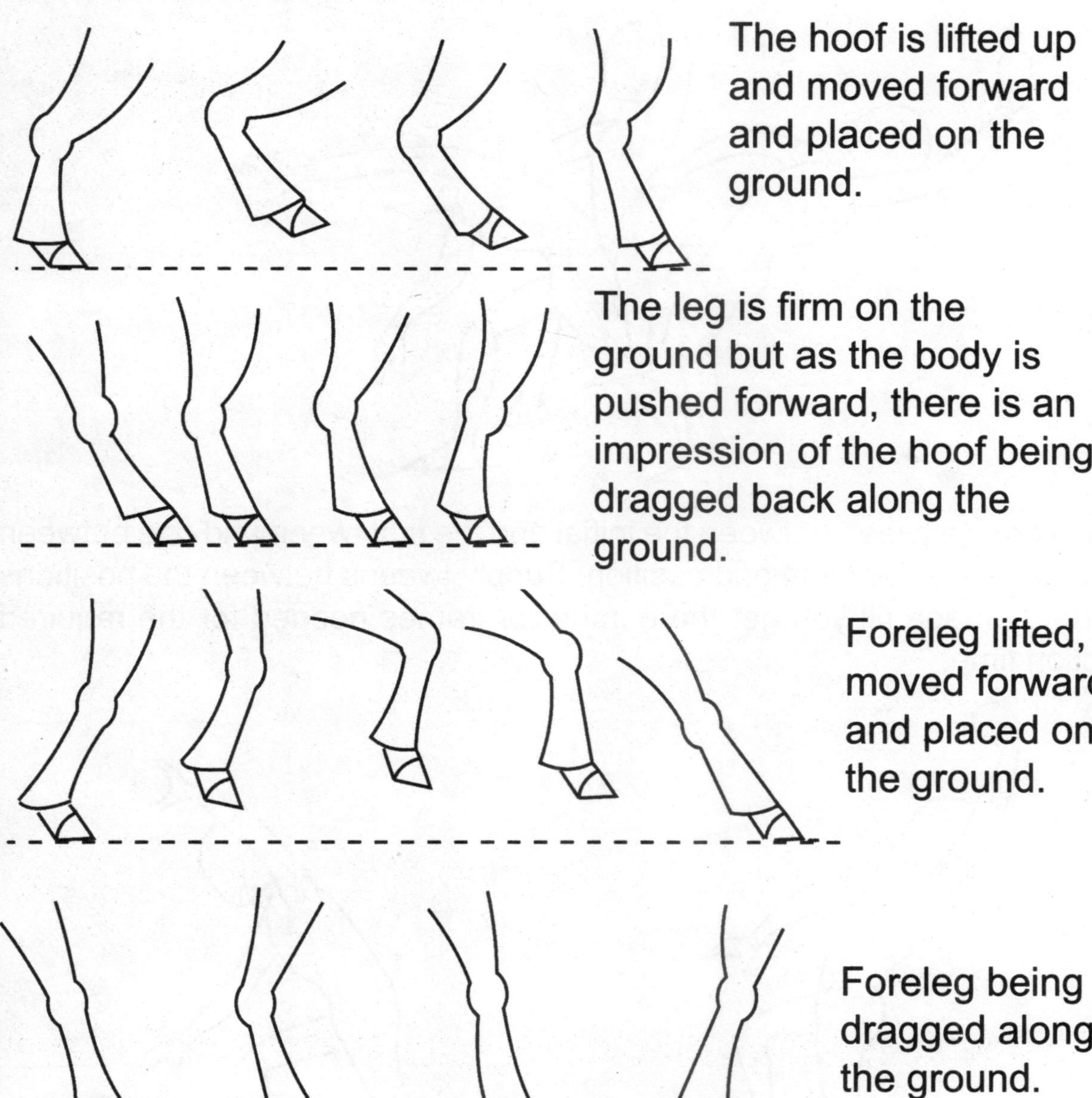

When capturing motion in a cine camera, tape or any other recording device, the image of the moving object is recorded in a sequence of frames. Each frame shows the object in progressive positions.

While animating, draw the initial and the end states, then draw the object in the mean position, that is the half way mark. This is the first tween (in between position).

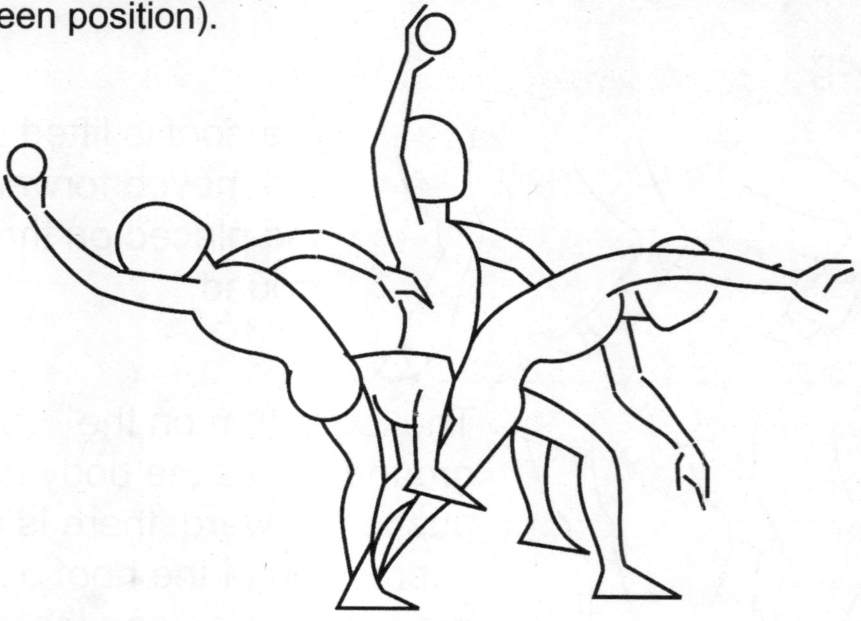

Now draw a tween between the initial and the first tween and one between the first tween and the end position. Supply tweens between the positions already made till you get the bumber of frames needed for the required action time.

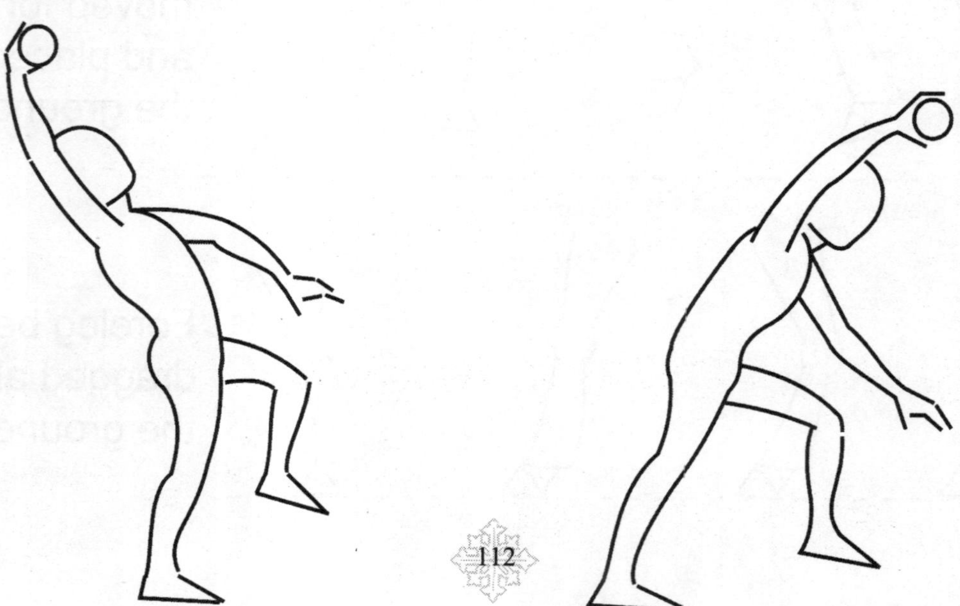

Marching
Walking
Jogging
Running

Making the characters turn is a tricky business. Your knowledge of solid geometry will be of help to achieve this. In the example below, a ball with a longitude drawn on it is shown in different positions as the ball rotates on a vertical axis from left to right.

When turning the chatacter, position the spheres (the basic components of the figures) in relation to one another – something like the motion of the planets. Mark the relevant longitudes and then add the details.

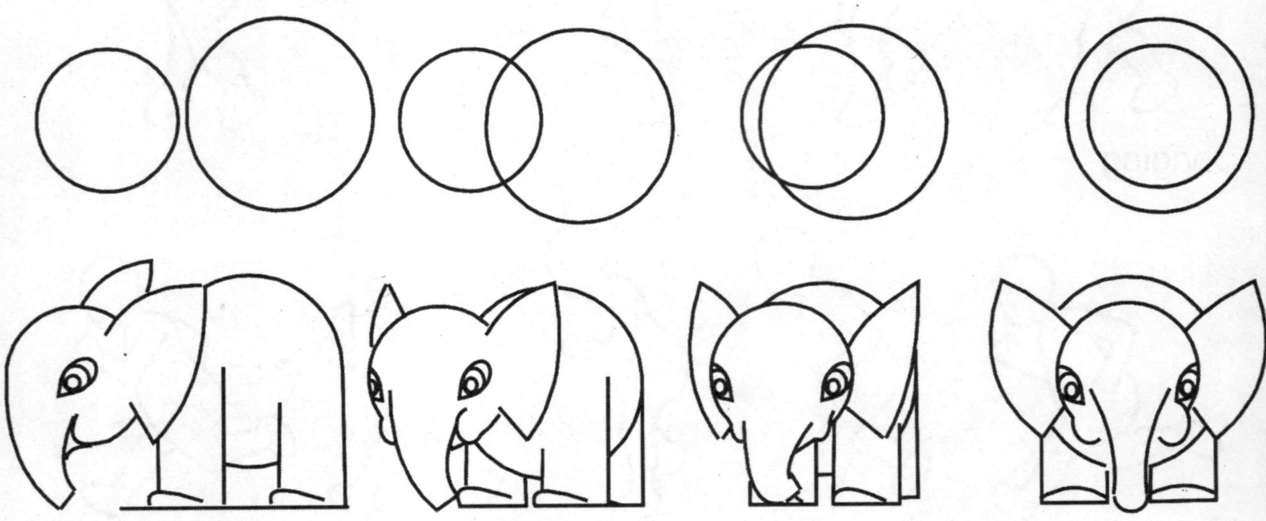

In animated cartoons, a fat person is very fat and an old person is very old.

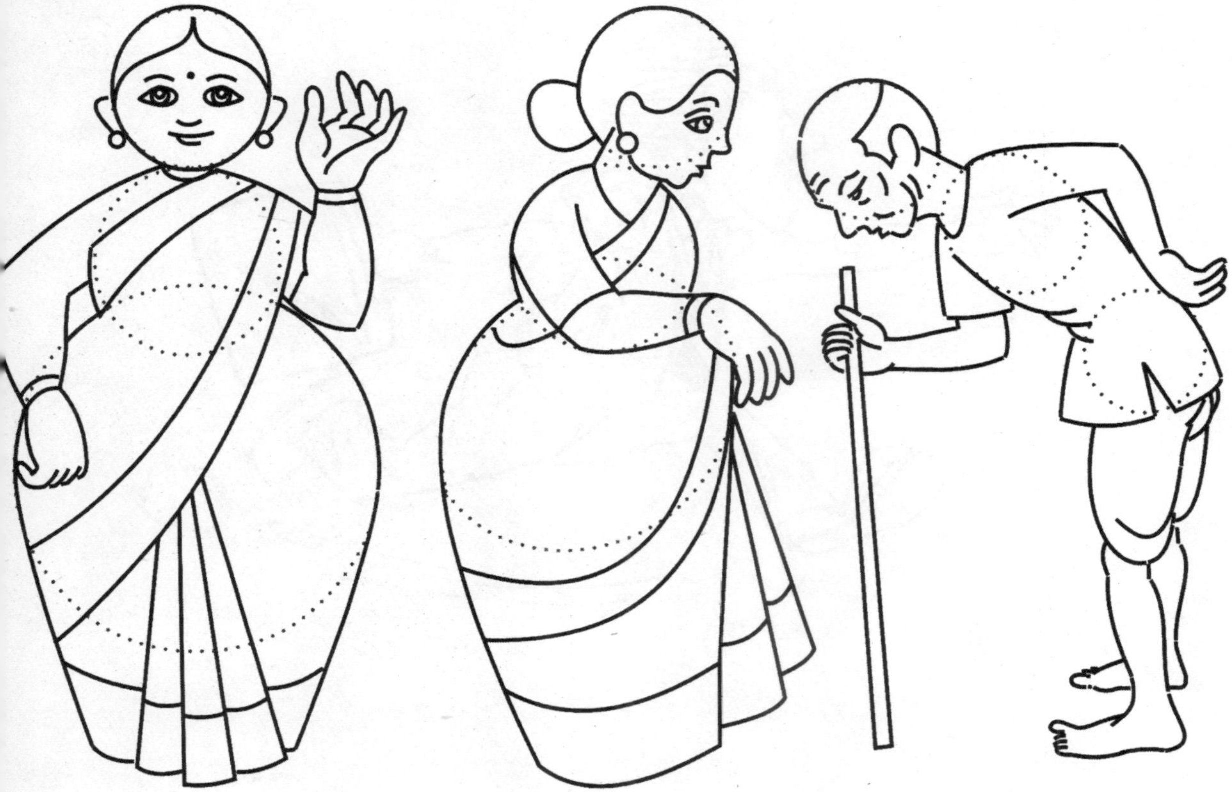

Use the skeleton to draw the above figures and draw them several times on a separate sheet of paper.

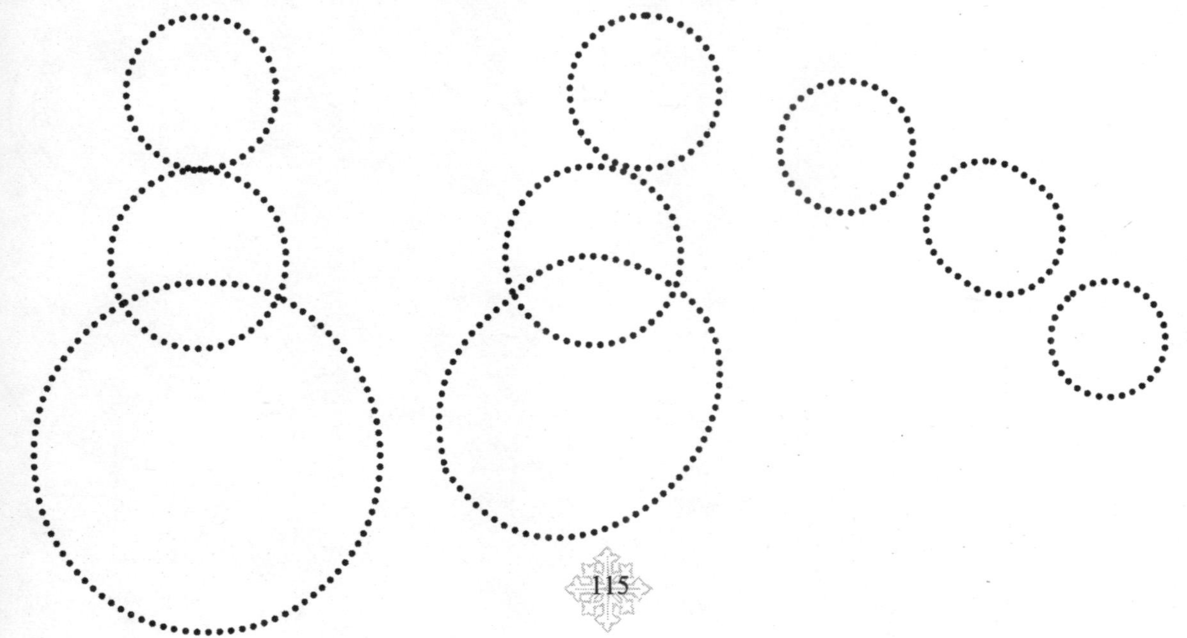